The Words I've Said

Poems and Stories Set Free from My Pen

Ted Harris

Copyright © 2019 by Ted Harris.

The Words I've Said: Poems and Stories Set Free from My Pen.

Printed in the United States of America.

All rights reserved solely by the author. The author guarantees all contents are original and do not infringe upon the legal rights of any other person or work. No part of this book may be reproduced in any form without the permission of the author.

Harris, T. (2003, September) "Someone Prayed for Me" in *Mature Living*, Vol 27, Number 12, 45. Reprinted and used by permission by Lifeway.

Harris, T. (2003, August) "Father-Child" in *Mature Living*, Volume 27, Number 12, 50. Reprinted and used by permission by Lifeway.

Photos of Dobbins Chapel courtesy of United States Air Force. Use of these photos does not imply endorsement from the government or the Air Force. U.S. Air Force photos by Brad Fallin.

All rights reserved.

ISBN: 9781709811425
Imprint: Independently published.
For World-Wide Distribution.

Author photo by Eric Schroeder.

Cover design and photo editing by Eric Schroeder.

Copy-editing by Désirée Schroeder.

DEDICATION

This collection of words, given to me by God, is dedicated to my wife Suzi, our daughter Dana, our son Hunter, his wife Catherine, and his daughters Carter and Spencer. They are the reason I live, laugh, and love. I hope these words will help them know who I am, who I was, and who and where I hope to be in eternity.

ACKNOWLEDGEMENTS

I want to express my special thanks and appreciation to Désirée Schroeder for editing, compiling, and putting this book together. And to her husband, Eric, for his photography and for his patience while his wife worked tirelessly to help us get these poems from notebooks, envelope backs, napkins, and various scraps of paper into a book. And to Sherry and Mike Anderson for their encouragement, energy, and all their efforts to get my works out of the storage box and into a book to share with others.
If it weren't for them this book would not be.

TABLE OF CONTENTS

DEDICATION I
ACKNOWLEDGEMENTS III
PART 1: LIFE 1
   WHAT WILL I BE? 1
   DO I HAVE WHAT IT TAKES? 2
   TO REFINE 2
   THE PEN 3
   THE BOY 3
   NO TOMORROWS 4
   DIRT ROADS OF MY PAST 5
   GHOSTS 6
   IF I COULD AGAIN 7
   UNCLE TRUETT 8
   BARN DANCE 9
   THE LIFEGUARD 11
   A BROKEN HEART 12
   LAST WORDS 12
   PROBLEM CHILD 13
   PUMPKIN VINE CREEK 14
   BLESSINGS 16
   LUCKY MAN 17
   GODLY FRIENDS 18
   THE WOLVES OF WORRY 19
   WASTED ANGER 19
   FATHER'S SINS 20
   IF YOUR CHILD 20
   THE BOTTLE AND ME 20
   SCARS 21
   IN A MORNING GARDEN 22
   COME ON 22
   ENCOURAGE 23
   A POTENTIAL MASTERPIECE 23
   I AM STILL 23
   PERSISTENCE 24
   WAS IT WORTH IT? 25
   LAST HUNT 25

GOD'S CONTROL	27
A TOAST TO STRIFE	28
MISSED CHANCE	28
CHURCHES	29
I WISH I COULD SING	30
LADY CLOWN	30
HERE BUT GONE	31
THE EYES OF JACOB WALKER	32
LOOKING	33
WENDALL RAY	33
DEATH HAS NO VICTORY	34
A WORKER	34
BOTTOM LAND	35
HOMELESS	35
THE TWELFTH STREET BRIDGE OVERTURE	36
EMPTY	36
BEWARE OF DOGS	37
FOOTBALL	38
THE SMILING-FACED CHERUB	40
PRIM AND PROPER	41
LITTLE BUTTERFLY	42
TWO BUMS	43
BEAUTIFUL FLOWER	44
FATHER - CHILD	45
HE WALKED WITH ME	46
TAPS	47
HOW LITTLE THEY KNEW	47
A YANK'S PRAYER	48
THE PAIN OF WAR	49
A YOUNG SOLDIER	51
DOBBINS CHAPEL	52
I'M PROUD	53
A CHRISTMAS THANK-YOU TO TEACHERS	53
DEAR SANTA	55
WILL SANTA COME TONIGHT?	55
CHRISTMAS AT THE BREWTON BUS STATION	58
CHRISTMAS GIFT	61
CHRISTMAS MORN	62
CHRISTMAS TREE	63
PART 2: LAUGHTER	**65**

IN THE CHURN 65
UNICORNS AND HONEST POLITICIANS 67
STRANDED 67
RAGS TO RUIN 68
SOUTHERN FINE 69
PEG LEG PETE 69
THE FIT 70
WRITE A RONG 70
HOP TOAD 71
THE BEST HUSBAND 71
USED TO COULD 72
POTATO CHIPS 73
THE BIG BANG 74
OPP ROMEO 74
THE TERRIBLE GERRIBLE 75

PART 3: LOVE 79

A MARRIAGE OF GOLD 79
FOR MY BRIDE 80
THE WINNER 80
WARMTH TO THE SNOW 81
FORTY-TWO 81
GOD BROUGHT YOU TO ME 82
MY VALENTINE 83
FOR THE 48TH 84
ME WITHOUT YOU 84
A KISS ABOVE ALL KISSES 85
YEAR FIFTY-TWO 86
FIRST LOVE 86
ONCE I DIDN'T LOVE YOU 87
SHE TOUCHED ME 87
WHEN I WAS YOUNG AND STRONG 88
HOLDING YOU 89
REMNANTS OF MY MIND 89
HER PRECIOUS MEMORIES 89
NO ONE BUT YOU 91
SHE GAVE 91
FOUND HEART 92
NEW LOVE 92
UNREQUITED 92
I WAS GOING TO SAY 93

DID YOU 94
SILLY MOON 94
IN MY MEMORY 95
HANDS 96
PATHS 97
TO BE OR NOT 97
THE WIDOWER 98
DUSTY OLD HEART 98
I LOVE 99
THE FRONT PORCH SWING 100
SMILE 101
FOREVER HERS 102
ONE MORE 104
FOR A LITTLE WHILE 104
LOVE WHEN YOU LIVE 105
FRIENDS 106
TELL HER 106
WORDS 107
WHO I WAS WHO I AM 108
TESSIE 108
THE KID 114
CHRISTMAS TREASURES 115
GIVING AND FORGIVING 116
THE OLD MAN'S CHRISTMAS 117
A STRANGE OCCURENCE 118
GOD TO MAN 118

PART 4: LIGHT 121

SET FREE 121
YOU SAW ME 122
THEY HUNG HIM THERE 123
A MOTHER'S POINT OF VIEW 124
THE HARDEST COMMAND 125
SOMEONE PRAYED FOR ME 125
HE CANNOT 126
THE INVITATION 126
PRODIGAL'S FATHER 127
HE ANSWERED WHO 127
A CARPENTER'S SON 128
WHEN STEPHEN WAS STONED 128
RAINS 129

REVIVAL	130
A HOMECOMING	131
PRAY AGAIN	133
THE PLANETS' LIGHT	133
PERHAPS SOON	134
THE MAN OF GOD	135
TALITHA KUM	136
COMFORTABLE	136
I'D RATHER	137
BLACK FRIDAY	137
CHRISTMAS FEELING	138
CHRISTMAS INVITATION	138
A CHRISTMAS POEM FOR DANA AND TERRY	139
THE FATHER'S CHRISTMAS GIFT	141
THE SHADOW OF A CROSS	142
THE TURNING TIDE	143
INDEX	**145**
ABOUT THE AUTHOR	**147**

PART 1

Life

WHAT WILL I BE?

What will I be when I grow up,
will I be tall as a tree or short as a pup,
will I love mustard and hate ketchup,
what will I be when I grow up?

What will I be when I am grown,
will I live on the street or have a place of my own,
will I be proud of the seeds I've sown,
what will I be when I am grown?

What will I be when I am dead,
just a name on a stone above my head,
or will people remember the words I've said,
what will I be when I am dead?

DO I HAVE WHAT IT TAKES?

Do I have what it takes, Daddy?
Am I yet a man?
Will I now or ever measure up?
Will you ever take my hand?
I know I haven't pleased you yet,
But you can still help me grow.
Do you think about me at all?
I so wish you'd let me know.
Am I becoming a man you respect,
Or only a bit of contempt?
Couldn't you once show me love,
Couldn't you at least attempt
To look at me like you do others,
With eyes full of love?
Or will I never receive approval
And the respect I'm dreaming of?

TO REFINE

Do not worry, do not fret,
God is not finished with us yet.
There's still a little grinding,
some rough edges have to go,
a few more dips into the furnace
to shape us and help us grow.
Just a little while longer,
our form to refine,
till He molds and makes us
to reflect His glory divine.

THE PEN

From within this pen
Flows forth ink,
Which writes words,
Sometimes before we think.
But these words can be stricken,
Or the pages thrown away,
But alas, this isn't true
About the words we say.
Every word we say to others
Can bring praise or pain,
So teach the tongue to only say
Those sweet, sweet refrains.

THE BOY

Where did that little boy go,
the one I used to be?
Is he still out chasing a rainbow?
Is he still up in a tree?
Does he still have a frog in his pocket
and bare feet in the dirt?
Does he still try to use humor

to hide from everyone the hurt?
Was he forced to become a man
by time's unrelenting ways?
Did he have to make all new plans?
Did any of his old dreams stay?
Has he found that life's gotten harder
and more difficult to understand?
Has he seen all of his dreams
silently slip though his hands?
Now as I shoulder another day
to fight the battles I need to win,
I wish somehow, some time, some way,
I could find that little boy again.

NO TOMORROWS

There is a truth in this cliché
we have no tomorrow
we only have today
yesterdays have gone
they cannot stay
all that we can do
must be done today

The problem with criticism I believe,
is that it is easier to give than to receive.

The words of a gossiper uncontrolled, falling fast,
destroy too many, too often, with the jawbone of an ass.

DIRT ROADS OF MY PAST

There was road dust on my toes
Granny beads below my chin
Oh, the simpleness of my childhood
I wish I could visit there again
Watermelon cooling 'neath the bed
Cicadas calling from the trees
My Granddaddy began to reminisce
As we gathered around his knees
Oh, the stories he could tell
He'd bring yesteryear to life
like how nervous he was then
When he asked Maw to be his wife
The cotton fields he picked through
The Alabama streams he fished
He said life for him had turned out to be
Harder than he had wished
He died when I was twelve
He just up and died and was gone
The song they played at his funeral
was "I Come to The Garden Alone"
It's the hymn I want played for me
When it's time for me to leave
But unlike I did then
I don't want my grandkids to grieve

We had a chinaberry tree
That for me was easy to climb
Where I'd perch and pretend
I was Tarzan in my mind
But the red light just changed now
As I'm brought back to today
And I must get back in traffic
Where I'll try to weave my way
I guess I'm just a day dreamer
Longing for the dirt roads of my past
And wishing for everyone I know
Our childhoods could forever last.

GHOSTS

I live on the old cemetery road,
in a shack by the mausoleum.
I know most don't believe in ghosts,
but I tell you folks, I see 'em.
Sometimes at night when the moon is bright,
and a chill hangs in the air,
I hear groans and the moving of stones,
and I know they're out there somewhere.
The cry of a cat, the flutter of a bat,
a shadow moves across the lawn.
I hear breathing and grinding teeth and
I know I'm no longer alone.
Like a misty fog rising from a bog
that swirls into shapes and forms,
the face of a ghoul, demonic and cruel,
bringing the darkness before the storm.
To my window I sneak to take a peek,
hoping they wouldn't see me.
Though full of dread, their dance of the dead
was something I had to see.
They swang and swayed, danced and played,
to a mournful spine-tingling tune,
while some of those there just floated on air,

painting ghoulish graffiti on the moon.
There was a stench in the air I could hardly bear,
as the night seemed to get much colder.
I thought I was safe in my hiding place,
then I felt a bony hand on my shoulder.
I jumped and cried, wanting to hide,
but the hand held me tight.
The hand shifted, and I was lifted
toward a glowing light.
I tried to kick but the hand was too quick,
so I started screaming and screaming and screaming.
Then soft as could be a voice said to me,
"Wake up son, you've been dreaming."
I opened my eyes and realized
I was at home, in my own bed.
And the horror I'd seen was only a dream,
there were no ghouls, demons, or undead.
It was Mom and Dad, and boy, was I glad,
although I felt a little foolish.
I told them my dream, how real it seemed,
so scary, so frightening, so ghoulish.
I hugged them tight as we kissed goodnight,
and they said that I would find
monsters and demons, of which I'd been dreaming,
were only in my mind.
And that I ought to think sweet thoughts,
to only let good things fill my head,
to pack my mind with thoughts sweet and kind,
and know that angels are guarding my bed.

IF I COULD AGAIN

If I could but go again
to those places from my past
to feel the warmth, taste the rain
and face winter's icy blast
the laughter, tears, and freedom
to walk another dusty mile

for me to be at the sea
that I loved so as a child
to lie on Grandma's feather bed
as the fireplace crackles warm
to hear at dawn the cock crow
or the tin roof in a storm
did these places and things exist
or are they figments of my mind
are they real or only a dream
that my heart hopes to find
perhaps they're things I've read about
or something I've longed to hear
but if they're false, how can it be
that they always bring a tear

UNCLE TRUETT

My mother's youngest brother was nothing but a man.
He could do the simplest things and make them seem grand.
He could even catch fish when the creek was dry,
And outrun a rabbit, and I think he could fly.
He used to take me with him.

And not once did he chide me and call me kid,
The way some fellows', I knew, uncles did.
But he talked to me about things like I was grown,
And showed me how to fix a flute out of a crow's wing bone.
And he always took me fishin'.

Lord, the slingshots that man would make,
Out of a forked hickory limb that nobody could break.
And that good ole' red rubber, you can't find anymore,
It'd beat any slingshot you bought in a store.
And when he'd talk, I'd listen.

I used to follow him around the yard, and he'd find things,
That little kids like me only found in dreams.
He found a practically new knife once and gave it to me.
But he could see things no others could see.
While I, sure as God's good, would miss 'em.

Sometimes we'd have many miles to walk, and being small, I'd get slow,
And he'd reach down to me, and before you'd know
I'd be on his shoulders, up there taller than kings.
And the songs about walking we used to sing.
Sometimes we'd join in some fancy whistlin'.

He told me about life and why we was poor,
And though we might never have money, there's one thing for sure,
If I'd walk tall in my life and follow God's plan,
I would never have to bow to another man.
And when I meet God, he'll be with Him.

BARN DANCE

My daddy played the flattop guitar,
My uncle played the steel,
While Buck banged on the catgut bass,
Its heavy thumping you could feel.

The nights were hot and heavy,
But the dancers didn't mind,
The moonlight and the moonshine
Had them feeling fine.

I was just a kid back then
Perched on a bale of hay,
While daddy called, "Change your partners,"
As they danced the night away.

THE WORDS I'VE SAID

Heavy brogans stomped the floor,
As southern girls with southern charm,
Tried to pace their steps just right,
To end up in the right boys' arms.

The Saturday barn dance socials
Still dance in the halls of my mind,
And bring me a kind of longingness
For a much simpler place and time.

Now we have cablevision and VCRs,
Entertainments at our beck and call,
There's restaurants, bars, and theaters,
I even sometimes do the mall.

The TV's available twenty-four hours a day
With various sports, weather, and news.
I'm faced with a myriad of distractions,
All I need to do is choose.

But if I really were able to choose,
The choice that comes to mind,
Is I'd want some magical way
To take control of time.

'Cause if time could be held in check,
Or the good days at least remade,
I'd like to perch on that bale again
When my daddy sang and played.

THE LIFEGUARD

The lifeguard throws the safety ring
tied to the rope
to try to save your life
to give you hope
Now, you can take the ring tossed
and turn your life around
or you can ignore the lifeguard
and stubbornly choose to drown.

A BROKEN HEART

A broken heart was here today.
Today, here, someone cried,
Because a soul had flown away,
Because someone had died.

They stood above the open earth
and tearfully questioned "Why?"
Though they know that from our birth
we all start to die.

And although death leaves such grief,
we really need to look
at death as not the ending
but a new chapter in life's book.

Now how that new chapter ends,
be it painful or be it nice,
upon you it all depends,
if you've written your book with Christ.

LAST WORDS

If I were told my time was short,
In weeks that I'd be dead,
I'd think of all the things and thoughts
And praises I've never said.

I'd gather up all good thoughts
To sing to family and friend,
To let them know what they've meant to me
Before I'd reached the end.

But why should I wait till it's too late,
If I've got praises to say,
My family, my friends, should hear it now,
… I think I'll start today.

PROBLEM CHILD

"My twenty-one-year-old son," I said,
"has an earring in each ear.
And to add to his appearance,
he wears his hair down to here."
The man I was talking to
didn't seem to hear or care,
so I continued, "Kids these days.
Weird clothes, weird ideas, weird hair.
The problems my kid has given me
I wouldn't wish on anyone."
I asked if he was stuck with such a problem.
He quietly said, "I have a son.
But my son is only five now.
Your problem is different from mine.
My son is fighting leukemia.
My problem is too little time.
To speak quite frankly," he said to me,
as his eyes glistened with tears,
"I'd love to know he'd be twenty-one
and have earrings in his ears.
I'd be pleased to know that as a teenager
we'd have our father and son fights,
and I'd give all that I now own
to know he'd be keeping me up all night.
But the doctors have pretty much said it's over,
my boy won't live to reach six."
Embarrassed and ashamed, I looked away,
His problem just couldn't be fixed.
"Your boy," he said, "will probably change
and make your old age happy and bright.
When I say my prayers with my son,
I ask the Lord, ... 'Is this the night?'
Rings in ears and hair that's long,
even attitudes change with time.
And I'd be proud to have your problem,
If you want to swap with mine."
He walked away and left me speechless,
Feeling very much like a fool.

And I thought about that boy of mine,
You know, he does look kind of cool.
So, Lord, grant me this prayer I ask,
give me wisdom and insight to see,
that long hair or short, rings or not,
there's still time that he will be with me.
We've made memories for twenty-one years,
and have a lifetime of memories to go.
And I know that I love him so much,
I think it's time that I let him know.

PUMPKIN VINE CREEK

Skipping stones on Pumpkin Vine Creek,
My Grandpa and me,
Checking the line from time to time,
Feeling lazy... Summer free.

School was still weeks away,
No need to worry 'bout that,
Grandpa and me had trot lines set
To catch a deep-water cat.

A kid can learn a lot it seems
From a grandpa at a creek,
Like why beavers dam the streams,
What language each critter speaks.

Or how to tie June bugs to a string,
Or make a flute from an old reed,
And to bake flour cakes on a hoe blade,
You know... stuff that all kids need.

But the best thing I got from him,
I guess that my grandpa ever taught,
Is that never ending, always forgiving love
Is something that can't be bought.

LIFE

He didn't teach it by preaching to me,
It was something he just showed.
He was simply a bottomless well,
Where the water of love overflowed.

Because through the years I'd mess up,
I'd leave his tools out in the rain,
Or forget to lock the barn door,
Or skip church again and again.

He just talked to me about responsibility
Toward church, family, and friends,
And that neglect and damage done to these
Couldn't compare to the hurt within.

When I thought I was almost grown,
Out at night giving the world a spin,
I might not get in till the rooster crowed,
He'd never jump me 'bout where I'd been.

He'd just say, "Are you alright, boy?"
With a kind of sadness in his voice.
"You know, life offers a lot to a man,
I'm praying you'll make the right choice."

He passed away a few years ago,
A couple of weeks before I was wed,
And now that I have a child of my own
I'm reminded of all that he said.

To say simple things like I love you,
Or, you can do it if you'll just try,
Help those less fortunate than you,
And always stand for what is right.

And take a kid fishing...
Make Sunday the best day of the week,
And make a flute from an old reed,
There's still a few at Pumpkin Vine Creek.

BLESSINGS

It seems I want what I shouldn't desire
or I desire things I shouldn't want
and when it comes to making good choices
somehow it seems that I don't
I attend pity parties
where I'm the only guest
and ask out loud, Lord
Lord, why aren't I more blessed
more than who He asked me
more than the man down the street
the one who drives a Cadillac
or the one who has no feet
maybe I could bless you more
if only I knew for sure
more blessed than the person
whose disease has no cure
maybe you'd feel more blessed
if I took some things away
like the job you complain about
I could bless you with no more pay
true your TV isn't a flat screen
but your TV picture is clear
I could bless you like some
who neither see nor hear
now your truck is truly old
about that we can talk
it could be new and shiny red
or perhaps I could have you walk
then I remembered a Bible verse
that was hidden deep in my heart
that says give me neither poverty or riches
God, only give me my part
feed me with only those things
that are portioned right for me
so I don't say look what I've done
and I deny your deity
or think that I am in need
and be tempted to take or steal
so forgive me, Father, for my blindness
I know that my blessings are real

LUCKY MAN

LUCKY MAN, LUCKY ME!
I have my wife and my family,
I have a job, I have health,
not much money, but great wealth.
I have dreams and answered prayers.
I have a friend who truly cares.
I have bruises, but still I see,
LUCKY MAN, LUCKY ME!
LUCKY ME, LUCKY MAN!
I can rest, I can stand,
and lend my neighbor a helping hand.
I have children who think I'm grand.
I can worship where I wish,
my cup runs over, God has filled my dish.
I know I'm part of His great plan,
LUCKY ME, LUCKY MAN!

GODLY FRIENDS

There is a man I know,
in fact, I know him well,
who felt that God deserted him,
that his life was bound for hell.
But his feelings were dishonest,
the words were telling him a lie.
He was listening to the mouth of Satan
saying, "Give up, give in, just die."
But because some godly friends
found out about his plight,
they reminded him of God's written Word
and joined him in his fight.
They reminded him of the truth,
and that Satan is a defeated foe.
Though he may stomp his cloven hooves,
with God's Word, we can make him go.
Jesus said, "I am with you always,
and I came to give you life."
So when Satan whispers out to you,
"You're a failure, I pity your wife,"
The man's friends said do as Jesus did,
and answer Satan with the Word,
which is the sword of truth,
and the other verses you've heard.
His friends again reminded him,
"Whether your problems seem big or small,
if money can solve all of them,
why, they're not really problems at all."
This man had health, a wife, and kids,
and friends who loved him and cared,
who knew when he needed a hand,
and took his burdens and shared.
So Satan take a tip from me,
if you want your plans to win,
you need to know you stand no chance,
with a man who has godly friends.

THE WOLVES OF WORRY

The wolves of worry are at my mind's door,
trying to fill me with great fright.
Snarling and quarreling, they snap at me,
determined to destroy my night.

But behind the door, I'm on my knees
recalling all the words I've read.
"Do not fear for I am with you,"
"Be anxious for nothing," He said.

A mighty fortress is my God,
My Rock, my Protector, my King.
And though the wolves batter harder,
they cannot break in while I sing.

What a friend I have in Jesus,
and I know my Redeemer lives.
So the wolves of worry finally retreat,
and I sleep in the peace that He gives.

WASTED ANGER

He was a small shriveled up man,
life to him had not been grand,
and the anger for him I had felt as a kid,
for something to me he one day did,
seemed to fade away at his very sight,
and the wrong he had done that I planned to set right,
had been accomplished by this man's fate,
there was now no need for anger, hurt, or hate.
There was only sorrow for the time I'd wasted,
the anger I'd had, the bitterness I'd tasted.
For, "Vengeance is mine, I shall repay,"
said the Lord to me, as He did that day.

FATHER'S SINS

I must pay for the sins of my father
For all the wrongs he's done
This I can bear
But, oh, the despair
That my sins must be paid by my son.

IF YOUR CHILD

If your child could see inside your mind
What do you think he would see
If your child patterned himself after you
What kind of person would he be
If you want to look at a reflection of yourself
Look down by your side
Think of this and remember the times
You drank, cheated, or lied
If your child could look into your heart
Would it find any love
If your child followed your paths
Would they be paths he's worthy of
So if you can't be the person
You would like your child to be
Try to do those shameful things
Where no child will ever see

THE BOTTLE AND ME

I never thought that it could be
but here we are, the bottle and me
what harm is one drink, or two, or three
we can handle it, the bottle and me
booze traps some people but I'm free
so say I to the bottle and me

it used to make me sleep so peacefully
but something's wrong with the bottle and me
my body aches and the things I see
this is our fate, the bottle and me
if it would let me go, just let me be
but now we're chained, the bottle and me
O, Lord God, have mercy and hear my plea
give me strength to push the bottle from me

SCARS

To hide the hurt and cover the scars,
I sought the salve of pubs and bars.
But no matter what I drank, or where,
The hurt and scars were always there.
I ran in the snow and danced in the rain,
As a way to try to release my pain.
But in the strongest rain or coldest snow
The pain was with me wherever I'd go.
I tried crowded parties to find my relief,
But the noisy laughter increased my grief.
So solitude's serenity became my nurse,
But in my aloneness I only grew worse.
I finally gave up, I knew nothing else to do,
So in desperation, my Lord, I called out to You.
You came and held me as a father does a child,
And said, "I've been with you all the while.
Your struggles, though painful, were a necessity
to get you to give up and see your need for Me."
Then I asked if He would hold me awhile,
And He opened His arms and gave me a smile.
And, oh, the love I saw on His face,
As my hurt and pain drifted into space.
He was like no one I had ever known,
He touched me, I looked, and my scars were gone.

IN A MORNING GARDEN

In a morning garden
I chanced to walk,
As I passed the roses
One said, "Stop and talk."

I walked on not speaking,
And I saw a mourning dove.
"Stop awhile and visit," said he,
"Let's talk of life and love."

But I hurried on quickly,
No waster of time am I,
So I never saw the roses grow,
Nor watched a dove fly.

Time is too precious to waste,
Only fools look at earth and sky,
But now it seems I have the time
While in my grave I lie.

COME ON

Come on, life... get better
come on, dream... come true
come on, heart... start healing
come on, sky... turn blue
come on, face... try smiling
come on, eyes... don't cry
come on, mouth... start singing
come one, courage... please try
please try a little longer
keep pushing until when
we find what we are waiting for
just around the bend

ENCOURAGE

Who was the first to pat your back
and say, "I know you can"?
Who was there the first time
you needed a helping hand?
Who first said, "I believe in you,
you can do it if you try"?
Who said, "Let me share your load,
you can aim for the sky"?
Who was there to encourage you
with an "Attaboy! Way to go kid"?
Maybe you have no answer,
because no one ever did.

A POTENTIAL MASTERPIECE

I'm between the potter's table and the kiln,
a potential masterpiece, with lumps.
There's still shaping and forming to be done,
some scraping away of all the bumps.
But I'm convinced when all is finished,
in beauty and glory I will stand.
A masterpiece I'll be, not because of me,
but because of the Master's hand.

I AM STILL

I am still broke
I am still writing rhymes
I am still searching
For my place and time

I am still confused
How to acquire luck
I am still hoping
For a pickup truck

I am still proud
Of both my wife and kids
I am still ashamed
Of some things I did

I am still excited that
I am still with my first wife
I am thoroughly convinced
God gave her to me for life

I am still dreaming
Of a place at the beach
I am still hoping
It will be within my reach

I am still seeking Jesus
And I think I always will
Until the Lord says it's over
And at last... I am still

PERSISTENCE

I watched a snail slowly crawl,
along and up an old brick wall,
part of a building being torn down,
to be replaced by what would be the pride of our town.
But the snail did not know this and crawled slowly on,
as the old wall quaked and died with a moan.
As the snail crawled on, a crack would appear,
but the snail crawled over it, never showing fear.
On he crawled until he reached the top,
then he paused to rest, I thought he deserved this stop.
But progress itself doesn't give in,

and the wall collapsed, the snail within.
Then I thought of the walls I'd faced,
the times I quit to avoid disgrace,
the times I'd take a slow and cautious pace,
never finishing on top, but always saving face.
Then from the bottom of this rubble and dirt,
the snail appeared, bruised and hurt.
It looked again at this pile of rock,
and started again to reach the top.
I thought, if a snail could do this, could find a way,
then I won't quit until that day,
I sit proudly atop the wall,
knowing persistence can do it all.

WAS IT WORTH IT?

It seems the times, the Ides of March,
are marching away with my life.
If all is weighed, and the rewind played,
was it all worth the strife?
Or were the loves I gained and lost,
all those steep rocky miles,
outweighed by my kids and wife,
all the snuggles, warmth, and smiles?
I'd have to say, when they carry me away,
and they tally my final score,
was it all worth it all,
I'd say, in every way, it was worth so much more.

LAST HUNT

The man pulled the cover over his son's thin shoulder and gently picked him up. The temperature was a windy thirty-eight degrees, maybe a little too windy for deer hunting, but he knew time was running out, and he had promised his son this trip if his son's condition improved. It unfortunately had gotten worse.

He walked on through the dark to a place where they could sit on a rise overlooking an oak-covered creek bottom, a place where several deer had been taken in the past. As he walked, he thought back to the times before cancer had riddled his son's body, when his son was strong, those times they would drive these bottoms, side by side, in hopes of kicking up the daddy of all deer. They had taken a few that way, but mostly they were just good times shared between a father and son.

He remembered the games his son had played at school – football, soccer, and track. He had loved sports. All sports. Now cancer was taking this young life from the father who loved him so much.

The cold wind was making the man's eyes water as he reached the spot he wanted to hunt. He sat his son down on the ground next to a blown-down black gum. The old roots, stuck high in the air, would give them a natural blind and would also cut the wind some. He loaded the rifle and laid it on his son's lap, and told the boy to rest, and he would look for deer.

As the sky began to turn that fuzzy shade of blue it gets early in winter, the boy said, almost in a whisper, "Do you think we'll see one?"

"We'll not only see one, we'll get one," his father answered as he patted his head.

A little after seven, they heard that old familiar sound of leaves being kicked aside by the slow steady pace of a buck.

Bucks, especially in rut, kind of swagger, dragging their feet. The father raised his son up and gave him the rifle. Minutes, that seemed like hours, passed before the buck, a nice six-pointer, appeared. The boy was having trouble holding the gun steady, and now seeing the deer this close made him tremble more.

His father said, "As he gets in that clearing by the persimmon tree..., take him."

The boy tried to hold a steady bead on the deer, but his weakened condition made it impossible. The father whispered to him to shoot as the deer came into the clearing. The recoil from the rifle blast knocked the boy back, causing him not to see the bullet strike several feet in front of the deer, sending the buck bounding off. He raised himself back up on one elbow and asked, "Did I get him?"

The father took the gun from his son's hands and started unloading it as he answered. "Yes, son, you got him. Looks like from here it's a good six or eight-point. I'll get you back to camp and send some of the guys back to get him."

The man picked his son up and started walking back to his truck. Lord, how he loved this child. The wind was starting to blow again as the man covered his son's face with the blanket and held him tighter, as if holding him would prolong the inevitable.

Snow had started falling as he loaded the truck and started home. Snow was falling later that week as his son was buried. He was buried on a hill at the edge of the cemetery overlooking a little oak-covered creek bottom, where a person could almost see deer feeding. It was the kind of setting where a man could take his son hunting.

GOD'S CONTROL

Nothing is by accident,
Nothing by happenstance,
Nothing for no reason,
Nothing simply by chance.
Nothing ever in our lives
Is not under God's control.
Everything is allowed by Him
To make us and to mold.
To fit into His eternal plan,
We're chiseled for each part,
To create the Bride of Christ,
To prepare, for Him, our hearts.
So when the potter takes the clay,
When the refiner heats the flames,
Until the dross and waste are gone,
... Until all that remains
Is a masterpiece by God,
Part of His eternal plan,
Where no two are ever the same,
A unique design by God's hand.
Just remember when all seems lost,
When all seems out of control,
Know that God has us in His hand,
Our heart, our body, and soul.

A TOAST TO STRIFE

If life was fair
Like we wish it was
And things were good
Well, just because
And we all had money
And our knees didn't hurt
Had T-bones for dinner
With apple pie for dessert
If we had all we wanted
No matter how odd
Then we wouldn't have
Any need for God
So here's to our problems
Our struggles and strife
Thank You, God, for providing
The need for You in our life

MISSED CHANCE

Sorry, Lord, but I was busy
when You came by today
I had so many errands to run
and a round of golf to play

I sure wish that I had been here
today when You dropped by
I was really on the run, though
my, how the time does fly

I know I should be ready
for You to stop and visit a while
but with the job, TV, and trips to the mall
just to keep up with the latest styles

I completely missed You today it seems
So, I hope it's not too late to learn
and that maybe I'll have time for You
Lord, if You ever return

CHURCHES

I heard two men talking
About their churches one day,
And I was deeply touched
By what one had to say.
The first said, "My church is
On the edge of town
High on a hill and
For miles around
It can be seen and
Draws people in,
And the congregation has
Most of the town's richest men.
It's a work of art,
None other can compare,
And everyone knows
That I go there."
The other said,
"My church is quite small,
And in passing you might
Not see it at all.
It's down in a hollow
'Neath moss-covered oaks,
And its attendance is
Made up of just common folks.
And our budget," he laughed,
"We never seem to meet,
So we give the preacher
Home-growns to eat.
And if anyone knows
I go there, I can't really say,
But it doesn't matter to me,
I just go there to pray."

I WISH I COULD SING

I wish I could really sing
strong enough to make the rafters ring
and ruffle the feathers on angel's wings
I wish I could really sing

I wish I could really dance
like Astaire or Kelly across the stage I'd prance
and put people in a trance
I wish I could really dance

I wish I could really pray
and knew the right words to say
to have things go my way
I wish I could really pray

I wish I could pray, dance, and sing
not for my glory, but for Christ the King

LADY CLOWN

With red shoes ten sizes too large
and a heart that's larger than that
painted on tears and a ball for a nose
and a high top velveteen hat

She acts the fool to make 'em laugh
she pratfalls to make 'em smile
she dances and cavorts around and around
she's dressed in the strangest style

She breaks her heart for others
so their broken hearts can mend
she's the perfect pick-me-upper
for those who've reached their end

She's so good at bringing them cheer
making them laugh again and again
because beneath the paint and makeup
she hides her hurt and pain

So what she needs, this sweet dear clown
is something I've always known
she needs to be able to remove her mask
and have a clown of her own

HERE BUT GONE

"Mama, it's me," I said
as I stroked her hair.
She didn't seem to notice
that I was even there.
"You look beautiful today,"
I spoke to her again,
and gently kissed her forehead,
and took hold of her hand.
Her cloudy eyes looked at me,
as if waking from a dream,
but this is a nightmare,
a reality nightmare it seems.
Alzheimer's is taking her from me,
just leaving this aging shell,
that once rang with laughter,
it reared and love me so well.
"Oh, it's me here again,
please be able to recognize"
and for a fleeting moment I saw
remembrance in her eyes.
Just as quick it was gone,
and she fumbled for her words,
"I'm not, I'm not sure who you are,"
was the painful response that I heard.
"Oh, how much I love you, Mama,
and I want you to know

I will be back tomorrow,
but now I need to go.
I still see you young and pretty,
bouncing me on your knee
at our special tea parties,
you and my dolls and me.
I pray that you aren't frightened
and that you can understand
that God loves you even more than I do,
and He has you in His loving hand."

THE EYES OF JACOB WALKER

The eyes of Jacob Walker are not silent.
If you watch them, you can hear them speak.
They say that one of us here has killed him,
one of us is the one he seeks.

The coffin still holds his silent body,
but his eyes, his eyes, I see speak.
He's dead, I know, I must be dreaming,
but is that a slight movement in his cheek?

We're gathered here to pay homage
to a man whose strength made us weak.
He knows which one of us killed him.
Oh God, don't let those eyes speak!

His eyes are talking directly to us,
he's telling the others I'm the one he seeks.
Yes, Sheriff, I'm the one who killed him.
You wouldn't have known it if his eyes didn't speak.

The others stand and watch as I'm taken
for his murder, they thought I was meek.
And they're shaking their heads in pity,
you see, they didn't hear his eyes speak.

LOOKING

Looking at those people
and the look upon each face
they are looking for someone
they're looking for their place
they're looking like lost ships
that are looking for the shore
they're looking like empty lives
they're looking for so much more
they're looking for a ray of hope
they're looking for a break
they're looking for a can of beans
they're looking for a steak
they're looking for an open road
they're looking for a way that's clear
they're looking for an I love you
they look... but never hear
they're looking for the strength to try
they're looking for a chance to be
and looking at them I realize
I'm looking at you and me

WENDALL RAY

There was a time that in our town there was a story told,
of a woman fair, whose silken hair was surely made of gold.
And in this town back in that time the story goes to say,
that all men loved and wanted this girl, but none like Wendall Ray.
Now what I heard and what I believed, I'll prove later on,
that Wendall's love for this girl, around the town was known.
But this girl, lovely as could be, was really quite cruel and cold,
and she played a game with Wendall Ray, a deadly game I'm told.
She led poor Wendall around that town, that town back in that time,
with fluttering eyes like butterflies, with kisses, laughter, and wine.
She told some others back there, that time, about the game she played,
and they all laughed and raised their glasses and toasted to Wendall Ray.
Here's to the fool, they all laughed, the fool is all they said,

THE WORDS I'VE SAID

and though they swore to keep her secret, the gossip and laughter spread.
Poor Wendall Ray, when he heard the news, knew he had nothing left.
So, he bought a gun, his only one, went home, and killed himself.
The story is true, I've seen the proof, I've even seen his grave,
and the golden hair of that woman fair is gray on a person who raves.
Wendall, she asks, *Wendall*, she raves, *Please forgive me, Wendall Ray*.
Her mind snapped when she heard the news, she's been broken since that day.
Some people think that justice was done, some think that it's not fair,
some even say, she believes Wendall Ray still strokes her golden hair.

DEATH HAS NO VICTORY

Grave,
I know where your sting is,
it has pierced my heart and pours out through my eyes.
Death,
you have no victory,
for now I realize,
she is not here,
but in heaven above,
with her heavenly Father and Jesus,
wrapped in eternal love.

A WORKER

He worked down at the local mill,
on their receiving dock.
For almost eighteen years
he punched their time clock.
He fell one day beneath a truck,
he died almost instantly.
The owner of the mill said, "What a shame.
Now, just which one was he?"

BOTTOM LAND

Tell him I changed my mind
I got a better plan
Tell him I don't need his job
I got cotton in the bottom land
Tell him I'm tired of his complaining
I've had all of him I can stand
I won't be clocking in tomorrow
I got cotton in the bottom land
Yeah, I got cotton in the bottom land
With bolls bigger than the head of a cat
I'll be getting 'bout three bales to the acre
Maybe buy me a new wagon or a Sunday hat
There's jobs you gotta keep to keep eating
To pay the banker, and the doctor man
But I hear good times calling, I'll do no more crawling
I got cotton in the bottom land

HOMELESS

The winter wind cuts through me, like a scalpel made of ice,
Forcing me to seek the warmth in the sunshine against the wall.
The people hurrying home from work are all probably nice,
But they don't seem to notice me or even care at all.
I tug on my old tattered coat, trying to hide my face,
Drowning out the moaning of the wind's lonely cry.
I know that when the sunlight finally dies in this place
Then tonight here sadly, all alone, so will I.

THE TWELFTH STREET BRIDGE OVERTURE

Like paper blowing down the street,
The wino weaves his way,
Begging pennies from strangers
To buy his strength for the day.

The will to live in him is gone,
He's a bitter beaten man.
When life unknowingly pushed him down
He simply failed to stand.

A lot of these men are at the Twelfth Street Bridge,
Where they've built themselves a nest.
There they drink their wine to sorrowful times,
Those times they failed life's tests.

This group of men, hollow and thin,
Sit together but are always alone.
And when they die... and they do die,
No one ever knows they are gone.

EMPTY

The thin, pale, little woman,
with sagging empty breast,
from too many children weaned,
too many years without rest,
with sunken, hopeless eyes,
long past the ability to cry,
said, "My old man wasn't much good,
still I hated to see him die."
Her family and friends rallied round her,
bringing what little food they could,
as she sat at the edge of his bed,
wondering why her life hadn't turned out good.
She touched the stubble of his beard,
his face snow-cold to the touch,

and said, "I'm gonna truly miss you,
even though you wasn't worth much.
Still these kids and grandkids
are here to help me get through,
and come to think of it, they wouldn't be here,
if it hadn't been for you.
You know, we never had it easy,
living for us was a constant task,
but these kids and grandkids you sired
are worth more than I could ever ask."

BEWARE OF DOGS

Do not love a dog
a dog will up and die
taking your heart with him
without even a goodbye
don't let one kiss your hand
or snuggle in your bed
run from them, hide from them
before they fill your head
don't look into their eyes
they will draw out your soul
never scratch them behind the ear
or take them for a stroll
dogs think they're your protector
and will chase away the dark
it doesn't matter their size
their bite is worse than their bark
but love one if you dare
become a fool just like me
knowing that when they do die
they will live forever in your memory

FOOTBALL

There are no smiles on their faces,
They only show fatigue,
And they know wherever this place is,
It's no longer little league.
Their throats feel like cotton,
Their stomachs feel like "yuck,"
They don't want to be forgotten,
So, with maybe a little luck,
They'll catch that pass, deflect the ball,
Block that punt, or score,
And show the coaches, one and all,
They're the players they're looking for.
They support themselves hands on knees,
Throwing up last night's meal,
Then wipe their mouths on their sleeves,
Reaching deep inside for the will
To run again one more lap,
And another and still another,
Then they all begin to clap
Football brothers encouraging brothers.
They crash into their beds at night,
Bodies tired and sorely aching,
Wondering if trying to play was right
Then sometime before the dawn's breaking,

LIFE

Comes the answer they can see,
Almost like in some prophet's dream,
"This game isn't to support me,
I'm here to support the team."
We may not all be backs or stars,
But we can all be part of the quest
To make this the best team by far,
If only we each will do our best.
And if our best doesn't always win,
If our team doesn't make the grade,
The other team will know it was a fight they were in,
And we'll all be better because we played.

Some people touch things and they turn to gold,
others touch things and they just mold.
Now I'm not saying out of these
which I am... but would you like some cheese?

Call it what you want
my destiny or my just fate
but this ship of life I'm riding
is sailing through the Dire Straits.

THE SMILING-FACED CHERUB

She was a smiling-faced cherub,
Always trying to please,
A bundle of girlish giggles,
Riding "horsey" on my knees.

She was a ballerina in pink,
Trying a pirouette on her toes,
A young girl who grew too tall,
To really have steady beaus.

She was a teenager on the beach,
Turning heads when she walked by,
Who'd learned to hide her feelings,
And to never, ever cry.

She became a stranger for a while,
Pursuing interests of her own.
I wondered for this brief time,
Was this the same girl I'd known?

She became a young woman,
Independent, on her own,
And in her independence,
She decided to return home.

She's a woman, beautiful and loving,
The very light of my life,
But she's decided the time is here,
To leave and become a wife.

She's going now, but I know,
We'll never really be apart,
'Cause she's left her mark forever,
In her dear old daddy's heart.

PRIM AND PROPER

Little Miss Prim and Proper
she's a real traffic-stopper
everywhere that she goes
her fan club just grows and grows
yet she's so proper and so prim
she's never even spoken to him
the boy who works at the store
who bags her groceries and opens the door
this prim and proper pretty lass
considers him below her class
and never in her wildest dreams
would date him and so it seems
a beautiful love will never start
because of a prim and proper heart

LITTLE BUTTERFLY
written for my granddaughters

Little butterfly so whisper-thin
Velvet dancer on the wind
Skipping from flower to flower
With your graceful gentle power
You're brightly colored bits of light
Shining bright for my delight
Yet it seems so strange to me
That a worm you used to be
Yes, just a lowly little worm
That on the ground would wiggle and squirm
And perhaps no one ever knew
The strength and beauty held in you
But now, so it would seem
You've awakened from some dream
To leave the earth far below
To soar wherever you want to go
To rise above all the rest
You opened up to become your best
Makes me wonder what could be
The strengths and beauty hidden in me
And I know if I will dream and try
There's no telling how high I can fly

LIFE

TWO BUMS

Two bums on the roadside sat,
And fanned themselves with their hand-held hat.
They knew the reasons, and often would chat
Over the fate of things, of this and that.

Smoke rings rung the old one's face,
As he told of the time of his birth and place.
"T'was good it was, it was satin and lace,
And for five hundred years my blood line traced.

"My every need was always filled.
I went as I wanted, and I wanted at will.
No price too high, I thirsted for thrill.
People I broke, even innocent and ill.

"My fate was cast before my birth.
I was rich, dastardly and ten times worse.
But I fell in love once, my last and first.
And since that time, I've been cursed.

"She threw me aside for a begger's son,
Not for what he could give her, but for what I had done.
Now I follow the wind where the freight cars run
Wanting my past deeds undone.

"But I'm old now, my eyes are dry.
I'm dying; I'm empty, but I don't why.
T'was my fate that did it to me, not I.
Were the Lord my Savior, He would tell me why."

Two bums on the roadside sat.
One turned and stood and put on his hat.
The other's still body lay quiet and flat,
And the wind whistled round him, and that, was that.

BEAUTIFUL FLOWER

I watched a flower fading away
at evening's dying light,
yet its beauty and fragrance remained
after it was gone from sight.

This gentle beauty had blossomed for years
bringing joy to all around,
giving strength to those weary in heart,
drawing laughter out of frowns.

I thought its loss would bring such sorrow,
more than my heart could ever tell,
but then I noticed something growing
... there where the flower fell.

A bright ring of new flowers
each with a beauty of its own,
was waiting to bless the world,
seedlings from the flower now gone.

I looked at this young bouquet
then smiled to myself as I
realized that the love in that flower
was still here and could never die.

FATHER - CHILD

I used to wipe milk from her mouth,
Now she's wiping milk from mine.
That was when we were both younger,
Seems like such a short, short time.
I used to wrap her with a blanket,
At night as she watched T.V.
But now my bones are old and cold,
And she tucks a blanket around me.
I used to hold her hand so tight
When we had to cross each street.
Now she softly grasps my hand
At every corner that we meet.
I used to check on her at night
And kiss her cheek so tenderly.
Now she helps me into bed,
And how tenderly she kisses me.
I used to teach her things I knew,
Like how to jump and skip and throw,
But now she has to remind me at times,
"Dad, this is someone that you know."
I used to be her everything,
A hero, her first date, her chauffeur,
But now it seems I would be nothing,
If it wasn't for her.
Time has a way of reversing roles
To where we're not what we seem to be.
I was the father, now I'm the child,
The one I cared for now cares for me.

I used to be someone long ago
That... well, I can't seem to recall,
But as I look into her loving face,
Whatever I was, was worth it all.

Reprinted and used by permission by Lifeway.

HE WALKED WITH ME

I didn't really appreciate him,
His soft words and gentle smile,
But I know my life is much brighter
Since he walked with me a while.

Our walk together now seems too short
I wish now I'd really heard
There were so many things he told me
At the time they were only words.

But these words have now become my strength
As I continue the lonely miles
And I know my life is much brighter
Since he walked with me a while.

LIFE

TAPS

The lonely sound of Scottish pipes
rolling softly over the bay
and the silent soldier blowing taps
at the closing of another day
speak of men everywhere
who have died in all wars' way
that makes me take my son and hold him
and hold him while I pray
dear merciful God, sweet giver of life
please pause and listen to me
war has killed so many men
so often and so needlessly
please end war before it's too late
he is still just a child, You see
and if those lonely pipes must play
then let them play for me

HOW LITTLE THEY KNEW

How little they knew of war that day,
When with wooden muskets they went out to play.
And if they knew more no one could say,
When one dressed in blue – the other gray.

Like two peas in a pod, their mama had sworn,
And few could tell them apart from the day they were born.
But on the trials of war, they had never been warned,
So with the innocence of youth they felt their country torn.

Ned, the younger by a minute or two,
Was visiting up North with a family he knew.
When the great war came, he put on blue,
'Cause being with them, what else could he do?

And his brother Ed, who was plowing their land,
Put on gray to take his stand.
They were in their youth, neither child nor man,
As Ned fought for an idea, and Ed his land.

And as fate would have it, the battle that day,
Had drawn them together where they used to play.
Across the fields of their home stretched blue and gray,
And in that field of death they both would stay.

Rifle shot and cannon fire made a deadly wall
That crushed men from both sides and drowned out their calls.
Ned, in sad confusion, stood there straight and tall,
And all memories of youth choked Ed as he saw his brother fall.

Blood's thicker than water, it's often been said,
This is true, Ed thought of his brother Ned.
As he sat down and cradled his brother's head
Crying, "Don't die, don't die!" – but he was already dead.

Blinded by tears and filled with defeat
Ed sat as he watched his lines retreat,
Removed his sword and stood to his feet,
Placed his pistol to his head and made the bitter sweet.

A YANK'S PRAYER

The coarse gray cold of dusk,
Stole silently through the field.
As we dug deeper in our trenches,
Wondering how many more men we killed.

And how many more would die tomorrow,
With the dawning of morning light.
But for now the guns have been silenced,
With the coming darkness of night.

Fear gripped me so bad I just sat and cried,
When through the darkness I heard a voice say,
"If anyone out there can hear me now,
Won't you please join me while I pray?

"Dear Merciful God, our Heavenly Father,
Please end this war tonight.
There's been too much death and sorrow,
Won't You delay the morning light?

"I have no hatred for my brothers,
Who fight on the other side,
And I believe, Father, they agree,
Too many young men have died.

"But if tomorrow's daylight does come,
And I must answer the battle's call,
I pray you'll take me home to glory,
If in tomorrow's battle I fall."

THE PAIN OF WAR

Sweat, heat, and flies,
covered us as we pressed on,
the point man, just yards away
felt always alone.
A shot rang out
just missing my shoulder
the point man fell,
his war was over.
"Do you see him?" Sarge yelled
as we hugged the ground.
"He's at three o'clock!" I shouted
and fired another round.
We checked him for his papers
then formed back together.
We had found a bag of rice,
and in it a crumpled letter.

THE WORDS I'VE SAID

Ching Lee, our interpreter,
read to us out loud
the letter that we found
that silenced our crowd.
He read, "Dear Son, though you're away,
and are fighting for a cause,
a war that is supported
by our leaders and our laws,
I just can't help feeling
that it has to be wrong,
but then, I am weak,
I know I should be strong.
But I miss you so much,
and I know if you could,
you would end this war today,
so be careful and be good.
I pray this war will end
so you can soon come home.
It's not good for your wife
or your son to be alone.
Speaking of your family,
you should see your boy,
he's nearly eight months old,
and just so much joy.
He looks a lot like you,
but he's got his momma's eyes,
and when we read your letters,
even he sometimes cries.
Please be careful,
and if God is willing,
this war will soon be over,
and there will be no more killing."
We all looked at one another
but didn't say very much.
This dead Viet Cong that
no one would touch,
had a family like mine
back at his home,
reminding me my wife and son
are also home alone.
We moved out then,

each feeling the pain
of war and misunderstanding,
of countries under strain.
Then another shot rang out
from somewhere up ahead,
and our protective platoon sergeant
rolled over dead.

A YOUNG SOLDIER

I saw his picture in the paper there,
He was a young soldier, lean and fair.
The picture was taken, so his folks said,
By a buddy of his who was also dead.
He left a wife expecting a child,
A mother and a father, they say he had his smile,
Two little sisters, and a dog named Blue,
Whose tail stopped wagging as if he knew.
Almost nineteen, the paper gave his age.
He was young, unknowing, but never afraid.
I read his letter, his folks were so proud,
He had been made private, they couldn't figure how.
His grandfather sat there never moving a bit,
With his gnarled old hands round the pipe he'd just lit.
Gladness showed in his fading eyes
When they read the letter where he'd won the prize.
The prize now sits on a shelf in the hall
That he'd won by being the best soldier of all,
Of all, that is, in his platoon
... Now his bed is empty in his room,
Except for a purple heart he'd won that day
Where he gave his life when he knelt to pray.
A sniper was watching everybody's child.
The bullet singled him out – he rolled and died.
The paper said he would be sent back home,
And I sit and cry, wishing I had gone.
The paper, his face, his family, his friends
... Not quite twenty – but he'd reached the end.

DOBBINS CHAPEL

This chapel may be small to the eyes of man,
But it is a giant in God's plan.
Born in the south to minister to a few,
But drafted to Europe in World War II.
How many it blessed who came through its door,
We may never know, but God knows the score.
When the war ended, I'm sorry to say,
It was dismantled, packed, and shipped away.
But this old chapel wasn't ready to quit,
There were new soldiers who had need of it.
And at Dobbins it finally found its home.
It's here to stay, never more to roam.
Thanks to the many who gave of their love,
Thanks to the workers, and thank God above,
Who knows that a chapel is more than dreams,
It's more than mortar, clapboards, and beams,
It's the very voice, the living word,
Where we worship, where our God is heard.

I'M PROUD

I'm proud to be an American,
I'm proud of the name I wear.
American – I'm American,
No other name compares.
I'm proud of my heritage,
I'm proud of the ones who died,
To pass on to me this country
That I now enjoy with pride.
I'm proud of our parents
And the wisdom they possess.
I'm proud of our children
And their youthful eagerness.
I'm proud to be in the mixture
Of a hundred different races,
Who may be of different colors
But are all American faces.
I'm proud of the opportunities
This country has to afford.
I'm proud of the thousand places
I can go to worship the Lord.
I'm proud of the love America shows,
And is showing everywhere.
It's in neighbors helping neighbors,
Or in a small child's prayer.
I know that it's been better said,
But if I'm ever allowed,
To say how I feel about America
I'll simply say – "I'm proud."

A CHRISTMAS THANK-YOU TO TEACHERS

I took my early morning coffee
and quietly sat down in my chair.
I looked at our Christmas tree
with all the presents waiting there.

THE WORDS I'VE SAID

It would soon be time to wake the kids,
but I enjoyed this moment of quiet,
as the tree's sparkling lights danced on the window,
casting colors into the night.

I was thinking about the Christmases past,
and I guess the ones yet to be,
and I thought of all the Christmas gifts
that had ever been given to me.

I remember the bike, the balls, and guns,
and, of course, all the new clothes.
I tried to choose my favorite gift,
if there was a favorite gift in those.

I placed my cup on the table,
stood up to take one last look,
when my eyes happened to gaze upon,
under the tree, a book.

This book I had given to all of us.
It was a collection of stories I'd read.
As I picked it up and thumbed the pages,
the characters came alive in my head.

This book, like so many others,
had at times really given me a lift,
and it dawned on me the fact I could read
was perhaps my greatest gift.

Some teacher, somewhere, some time ago
with patience and skill and time
taught me to read and opened my world,
gave me access to my mind.

And not only read, but to write and think,
and work math beyond two plus two.
I know the gifts my teachers gave
will last me my whole life through.

So, Merry Christmas to all my teachers,
I wish you could hear me say,
thank you for the time you gave me,
I still use your gifts every day

DEAR SANTA

Dear Santa, bring me a doll with lots of clothes
and lots of packages tied up in bows
and for my brother a cowboy suit
and a pistol with lots of caps to shoot
and Mom and Dad fewer bills
with greater health and no more ills
and last but certainly not the least
bring this world everlasting peace

WILL SANTA COME TONIGHT?

The little boy asked his Mama,
Will Santa come tonight?
She didn't want to break his heart
so she just said he might.

"You know, Mama," the little boy said,
"he's never come to our house before
and there's so many things I'd like to have
but only one I'm wishing for."

"What would you have Santa bring you?"
she asked, trying not to cry.
For she knew no matter how small the gift,
she didn't have the money to buy.

THE WORDS I'VE SAID

"You know I'm six and don't need much."
She heard her sweet child say.
"But Bobby's three and Mandy's four
and they still love to play.

"So I'd have Santa bring Mandy a doll,
a doll that could really talk.
And Bobby would get some cars or a truck
or a toy dog to take for a walk.

"But what I really want most of all
is to not ever see you cry.
I'd ask for my Daddy to get all better.
I don't want my Daddy to die.

"So Mama, will Santa come tonight?
I've been a good boy all year long."
She hugged her son and softly wept.
How could the world have gone so wrong?

How could the man she loved so much
be so sick, oh it had to be a lie.
But the doctors all told her the same story
before Christmas her husband would die.

But Christmas would be tomorrow,
and though her husband was still hanging on,
she knew the morning would be unbearable
with no toys and her husband gone.

She tucked her son in for the night
and went up to her room
where her dying husband's almost still breath
sounded the call of doom.

She knelt by his side and kissed his cheek
and laid her head against his chest.
Oh God, how she loved him and wanted him to live,
but the doctors had done their best.

LIFE

She closed her eyes and thought of Christmas
and the gifts she couldn't give.
How could she keep her children happy?
If only her husband could live.

She must have dozed for a moment or two,
'cause she woke when she heard someone speak,
and she was still kneeling by the bed,
with her lips against his cheek.

"Get up, Mary," the voice said again.
She turned but saw no one there.
All she saw was a trail of snowflakes
leading from the chair.

She followed the trail of melting snow
out the room, down the stairs and hall.
And standing where their tiny tree had stood
was a Christmas tree ten feet tall.

And the room seemed almost ready to burst
from the toys and candy and games.
And her children were in there laughing and playing
when they heard someone call their names.

"Mary, may I come down and join my family,"
said the voice they all loved so much.
And there stood her husband reaching out
with those hands she loved to touch.

They all cried and ran and kissed him
and he said, "Don't cry I'll be all right."
And as he hugged and kissed his wife and children
they knew that Santa had come that night.

Some people called what happened a miracle.
Some said it happened, well, just because.
But me and others who believe in Christmas
Know it was Santa Clause.

CHRISTMAS AT THE BREWTON BUS STATION

"Well, folks," the driver said as he pulled in next to the station doors, "better late than sorry – I mean, better safe than sorry."

Late is not better, I thought, *it ain't even good, especially if you've got to be somewhere on time.*

It was sleeting as the bus pulled into the Brewton Bus Station. It was late and very cold. The bus driver had driven slower than normal due to the icy conditions. It seemed like hours that I had been staring into the night looking for the lights of town. I heard the familiar sound of the air release as the door opened.

Mama was tired, I know. We had bought only two tickets for Mama and me and my little sister. My sister was only four, but she was a lapful for Mama, especially on a long bus trip.

We left Pearl, Mississippi around noon. We were going to my grandma's for Christmas. Mama had tried to get time off from her job but couldn't, so we were leaving on Christmas Eve and would have to come back the day after Christmas.

But Mama, who had a way of hiding her aches and hurts behind a smile, said, "One day, specially Christmas Day, at home with folks who love you is worth a few hours on a bus."

I know my Mama missed her folks a lot. My daddy had left us in Pearl, Mississippi to find his fortune and then come and get us. I guess he never found it 'cause he never came back... or called... or wrote... or anything. So, here we were in Brewton, Alabama, on our way home. We were supposed to change buses for the ride to Opp another seventy miles away.

Mama asked the driver, "What time is it?"

"It's ten forty," the driver said.

"It can't be that late," Mama said. "The bus to Opp runs at eight in the morning and ten at night. It just can't be that late."

Mama hurried us into the bus station. It was cold and bare. There were several wooden benches and, in the center, a big pot-bellied stove that heated the room. The man who worked nights there rubbed sleep from his eyes as he came into the ticket booth.

"Has the bus to Opp already gone?" asked Mama.

"Yep, little lady. Left about fifteen minutes ago. It waited a while, but because of the weather being bad like it is, they left."

"But," Mama pleaded, "we've got to get home before Christmas!"

"I'm sorry ma'am," he said, "but maybe you can go in the morning."

My little sister, who was just waking up, started to cry. "But what about Santa? How can he come? He can't find us here."

LIFE

Wow, I thought, she's right. I didn't like this one bit. I'd spent the last few weeks deliberately being good.

"Mama," I asked, "is she right? Can Santa find us?"

Mama said, "Don't worry about it. I'm sure he'll leave you your presents at your grandmama's house. You'll just have to get them later."

"I'm sorry ma'am," the ticket man said again. "I'll build up the fire in the stove and get y'all some quilts. These benches are hard, but this is the best I can do."

We took the old quilts he gave us and gathered round the stove. The bus ticket man threw in some coal and several pieces of stove wood. Soon the belly of that stove was glowing red. Mama made us as comfortable as we could be on the benches, but benches don't make good beds.

It was after I lay down that I noticed him, an old man sitting off to one side. He had a huge leather suitcase covered with stickers from places his travels had taken him.

He looked like someone's, or maybe everyone's, grandpa. He was resting his feet on his suitcase with his head leaned back against the bench. He smelled like Prince Albert Tobacco and had a stub of a pipe clinched in his teeth. He glanced at us briefly but seemed to be more interested in reading his paper.

My little sister was lying with her head on Mama's lap and crying softly. "We won't have Christmas," she sobbed. "Santa can't find us here."

"Hush, child," Mama said. "Even if he doesn't come tonight or tomorrow or next week, I promise you he'll come. Now try to go to sleep."

I thought to myself, *there's no way I can sleep on this hard bench*. Besides, I didn't want to show it, being older and everything, but no Santa and no presents on Christmas morning was something I dreaded. So, I concentrated on the glowing belly of the stove and listened to the crackle and occasional pop of the fire.

Mama was softly singing, "Go to sleep, my little angel, mine."

No way, I thought, *will I get any sleep tonight. No way!* But the warmth of the quilts and the stove overcame the stiffness of the bench, and I dozed off. It seemed as if I was dreaming, but I thought I heard the scuffle of feet beside me. I peered up from under my covers. The old man was moving from me over toward my sister. For a second I was frightened. *What was he up to?* I thought. *If he grabs my sister, I'm screaming for Mama*. But he only paused by her for a second or so and turned and picked up some stove wood and added it to the fire. He went back and lay down on the bench he had been sitting on. I didn't make a sound, but I didn't trust him. I was going to watch him the rest of the night. After all, I was the man of the family.

"Mama. Mama!" my sister shouted. "He came! He came!"

THE WORDS I'VE SAID

I opened my eyes not sure where I was, then remembered I was in the bus station.

"Who came?" Mama said.

"Santa came. He came, Mama! Santa found me!"

I looked at my sister as she was dancing around the room, twirling a small rag doll with button eyes and a sewn-on smile. Around and around she danced in the morning light, which streamed through the windows.

"Why? What?" Mama was barely able to speak.

Then I noticed on the bench, by my head, a baseball glove, a brand-new Rawlings leather baseball glove. The smell of the leather was like heaven. "Mama," I croaked. I could barely get it out. "He did come! I don't know how, but he found us."

Now, I know some of you think these were things that Mama had brought with her. But she couldn't have. First off, I helped her pack and there weren't any presents to be packed. And second off, I knew she had to pawn her wedding ring to get just enough money to buy the two tickets.

I looked around the room, and the old man was gone. His old suitcase with all its stickers was there, but he was gone. About then, the bus ticket man came in and said the weather had cleared, and our bus would be leaving at eight o'clock on time. Grandma's house was only a couple of hours away.

"Where is the old man?" I asked.

He said, "I think he walked down to the café for breakfast. You folks won't have time to go for breakfast, but I got some fruitcake and milk you can have before your bus takes off."

The Christmas sky was beautifully clear and bright. It was still cold, but the rain and sleet were gone. The bus ticket man, I guess because it was Christmas, let us have three seats on the bus for the rest of the trip. So, there we sat, Mama and my sister, rocking her new baby doll, in front of me. I had the seat by the window like always.

I looked out at the town as the bus eased out into the street and started moving along.

I could see the café sign up ahead at the corner. As the bus stopped at the corner, I saw the old man coming out from his breakfast. I pushed my face against the window to see better. It was him, sure 'nuff. He had that stub of a pipe clinched in his teeth. He saw me looking and, you won't believe this, but he laid a short stubby finger by the side of his nose and gave me a wink.

I couldn't hear him, but I could tell he said, "Merry Christmas. Merry Christmas to all," as the bus turned the corner. I then lost sight of him.

As we moved onto the highway, and picked up some speed, I looked at the new glove on my hand and then back toward town. *It couldn't have been,* I thought, *he couldn't have been... Could he?*

CHRISTMAS GIFT

Long before I was born
Before my parents even came to be
God in His great goodness
Gave a Christmas gift to me

My first Christmas present
So pink and soft and frail
Wasn't a gift for me only
But the entire world as well

It wasn't a toy or coloring book
A cap pistol or a knife
It was a little baby boy
The door to eternal life

God gave His Son as a baby
To feed at his mother's breast
To grow as a boy like I grew
To be challenged by life's test

My gift grew to be a man
Who was degraded, beaten, killed,
And though He could have changed things
He always did His Father's will

He knew the only hope for me
To escape the grasp of sin
Was for Him to bear my burdens
To die and then rise again

I can't speak for others
But I'm humbled at the sacrifice
That God in His great goodness
Gave me the gift of Jesus Christ

He died for everyone on that cross
But mostly He died for me,
So He could go and prepare a place
Where we'll fellowship eternally

Long before I was born
Before all the sins I've done
God in His great goodness
Gave me a gift... Christ Jesus, His Son

CHRISTMAS MORN

9:57 on Christmas morn
knee-deep in paper torn
from presents that shortly ago
were neatly wrapped and tied with a bow

makes me lean back now and sigh
and blink a tear from my eye
this is what Christmases are of
family, ribbons, toys, and Christ's love

CHRISTMAS TREE

Now I am not given to flights of fancy
my feet are firmly planted on the ground
but I believe I heard my living room cry
today when I took my Christmas tree down

Part 2

LAUGHTER

IN THE CHURN

Two frogs fell in a churn,
as you probably know,
and started to sink
in the milk below.

The first one said,
"There's no need to swim,
we'll never be able
to reach that rim.

"I'm giving up
without a single stroke."
As you might guess,
the first frog croaked.

The second frog said,
"I'm going to swim,
I don't want
to wind up like him."

So, around the churn
he began to go,
he frog-kicked,
smooth and slow.

But soon he tired
and began to sputter,
when he noticed floating,
large lumps of butter.

Encouraged by this,
he swam on and on,
till there was enough butter
for him to climb on.

He rested a moment,
then gave a big hop,
sailed from the churn,
and landed kerplop.

He shook himself,
and hopped on along,
looked back at the churn
and croaked a song.

Now the moral of this,
that you should learn,
is if life ever dumps you
into a churn,

Remember these frogs,
and never ever quit,
Take the problem you face
and make butter of it.

UNICORNS AND HONEST POLITICIANS

Unicorns and honest politicians
wherever did they go?
Or did they really ever exist?
It's what I want to know.
On elves and fairy princesses
I've always had my suspicions,
that they're only figments of the imagination
like an honest politician.
Now, politicians are verbose bundles
of handshaking promises and lies.
Who, if the truth were really told,
never told the truth in their lives.
But we get to elect them,
it's a democratic right we've won,
so we can watch our honest politicians
riding unicorns off into the sun.

STRANDED

Between virility and senility,
it seems I have been stranded.
I'm weather-worn and kind of forlorn
from all the tasks I've been handed.

The callouses on my hands
don't compare to the ones on my heart.
I still have some get up and go,
I just have trouble getting it to start.

The things I used to do all night,
now take all night to do.
It used to be Taco Supreme,
now it's milk and a prune or two.

THE WORDS I'VE SAID

Like a graceful galloping gazelle,
down the road I'd leap and bound.
Now, when I walk that road,
my feet barely leave the ground.

Sometimes a young miss smiles at me,
making me think I'm still quite cool,
till I hear her whisper to her friend,
bless his heart, that old fool.

But if a person lives long enough,
and survives most of life's tests,
having experienced both virility and senility,
I can't say which one is best.

I know they are all parts of living,
each having its own rewards,
makes me glad no matter where I'm stranded
I am here with my Lord.

RAGS TO RUIN

This is the story about my undoing
an inspirational work called "From Rags to Ruin"
it's about a poor but honest, hardworking lad
who learns to take the bitter with the bad
it's the story of a courageous, hardworking soul
who when finally on the bottom fell into a hole
about being compassionate, friendly and warm
and that it's always the blackest before the storm
about how a person with no money and yet
through struggle and planning winds up further in debt
it's a moving saga that will make you think
um, *would* think that is, 'cause I'm now out of ink

SOUTHERN FINE

Everything Southern is so, so fine,
We use Dixie Cups to drink our wine.
We love our chicken, Southern fried,
SEC football – Yeah, Roll Tide!
We have stone-ground grits slowly cooked,
Side of crispy bream we've just unhooked.
We love holding hands on a porch swing,
Or gathering round the campfire in a group sing.
I've been from Texas to the Georgia coast,
I've been a guest, and been the host,
Traveled from PC Beach as far north as Tennessee,
Seen it all, and it's very clear to me,
There is no place on God's great earth,
That can have any greater worth,
Than what we have here in the South,
'Cept for maybe these gnats crawlin' round my mouth.

PEG LEG PETE

Now Peg Leg Pete the Pirate
an unlucky cuss was he,
lost his leg below the equator
just above the knee.
He decided he would take a swim
and cool off in the sea.
This brought to Pete such sorrow,
but to a tiger shark great glee.
He was swimming and splashing,
floating on his back,
when a tiger shark came wandering by,
looking for a snack.
Now scientists say if a shark bites you
it's an accident no doubt,
and once they taste you're human,
they quickly spit you out.
Well, this didn't mean much to Pete,

it was all too personal to him.
Rarely again did he ever bathe,
and never, ever did he swim.
He just sat on the dock with a cup,
where he went daily to beg,
And to every sailor who came ashore
he asked, "Have you seen my leg?"

THE FIT

I know you'd have a conniption,
Or throw a hissy fit.
Or have a temper tantrum,
You wouldn't like it one bit.

You'd spew and spit and stammer,
Hold your breath till you turned blue,
Jump and jerk, maybe go berserk,
Like any caring person would do.

But Mommie, I'm a grown man.
I can choose who will be my friend.
And I'm going out to meet her now,
If I may have twenty dollars to spend.

WRITE A RONG

To write a rong
When it cumes to spellin
Chek the dicksonary
Cause theirs no tellen
What all you fine
What you mite lurn
And with good gramer
All the prayses yule urn.

HOP TOAD

I'm a little hop toad
short and green
I'm darn good-looking
and my wits are keen
I swims till I'm wet
and I suns till I dries
Just lying on my back
Catchin' those flies

This hung on our refrigerator for many years. It was even once turned in as a school assignment to find a poem that you liked. They said it was by "author unknown."

THE BEST HUSBAND

This morning for you, my sweet
I aimed carefully and lowered the seat
This is expressing this love of mine
for you, my Valentine
Another example of love no doubt
is I opened the door as you took the trash out
And I was patient as I watched TV
while you fixed breakfast for me

THE WORDS I'VE SAID

and to show that I love you a bunch
before you left for work, I fixed your lunch
and I waited all day by the phone
in case you needed to get something on your way home
and your second job is demanding, too
so, though it's late, I still wait up for you
I'm probably the best husband of all time
'cause nothing's too good for you, Valentine.

USED TO COULD

In the recesses of my memory
are glimpses of my childhood
makes me wish I could now do
things like I used to could

Life seemed to be much brighter and lighter
most of the time I felt real good
kinda sad that now I can't do
all the stuff I used to could

I could climb and run and jump
all over our neighborhood
now my running and jumping is nothing
like I used to could

I was just your average kid
neither too bad nor too good
my temperament now I can't control
like I used to could

Oh well, I guess in growing older
some things are just understood
we can't expect to do anything
like we used to could

POTATO CHIPS

"Tell me the answer, Old Man of the Mountain,
to the question on everyone's lips.
What is the secret of eternal life?"
He answered, "...POTATO CHIPS!"

Now that's ridiculous, I thought,
but I respected this so-called sage,
and said, "'POTATO CHIPS' is the answer
to the question of the age?"

He winked and squinted and looked at me,
his dignity he tried to compose.
He said, "If POTATO CHIPS isn't the answer,
well goodness, God only knows."

My wise old sage had let me down,
it was shattering to my youth.
"POTATO CHIPS" was his stupid answer,
I was looking for the truth.

I left the mountain a little bit shattered,
the one I trusted was so unreliable.
Where could I go, whom could I trust?
I found out in the Bible.

The Bible itself is a simple book,
full of questions and answers and love.
And there all my questions were answered,
were answered from above.

To think of all the mountains I climbed,
the toil, the trouble, the price,
only to find my heart's greatest questions
were easily answered by Christ.

THE BIG BANG

With the Big Bang Theory
there's really only one catch,
There may have been a big bang,
but... just who lit the match?

OPP ROMEO

I would climb Sand Mountain
Swim cross "Lite-erd Knot Creek"
There's nothin' that I wouldn't do
For the girl I seek
I'd buy her an RC Cola
Shuck her a dozen ears of corn
Give her a new coon dog puppy
If and when one gets born
Now there's nothing I would not do
For the girl I seek
'Cept, Roll Tide is kicking off
She's gonna have to wait till next week!

For those not fortunate enough to have been a child in Opp, AL, Sand Mountain was, in my memory, a place off an old dirt road where we loved to go play. Lite-erd Knot Creek, often spoken of as a great fishing place, runs between Opp and Andalusia. When I revisited these places as an adult, Sand Mountain was just a tiny pile of Alabama sand, and it turns out that Lite-erd Knot is actually spelled Lightwood Knot.

Prepare for Satan with the Word and prayers,
so you won't get caught in your unawares.

I probably shouldn't do it
but I feel I must complain
the light I saw at the end of the tunnel
turned out to be a train.

I don't know who to belly-ache to
to kick or cuss or thank
but when my ship finally came in
it immediately sank!

THE TERRIBLE GERRIBLE

The Terrible Gerrible comes to town
Every year about this time,
To try to eat all the Christmas candy,
And to rewrite Christmas rhymes.

A plate of candy left unguarded
Will mysteriously be gone.
And a poem rhyming *mitten* and *kitten*
Will have *mitten* rhyming with *moan*.

So, I decided to set a trap
And catch this thief myself.
So, I made some hollyberry fudge,
It's the favorite candy of an elf.

THE WORDS I'VE SAID

And I placed it on the windowsill,
Pretending it was there to cool,
And I hid nearby dressed like a bush,
I'm sure I looked like a fool.

But the Terrible Gerrible would soon find
This would be the last candy he would take,
And no more poems to my wife would he change
From being *in love* to being *in the lake*.

So, there I sat that Christmas Eve,
Prepared to spring my trap.
But it was late, and I was tired,
So, I took a little nap.

Next thing I knows I hear a racket,
Like someone's on my roof.
So, I runs out to the middle of the street,
I wanted to have some proof.

Well, what I saw you wouldn't believe,
It was sure 'nuff Santa himself,
And I thought, *Oh my goodness, I'm not asleep!
If he sees me, I won't get anything left.*

So, here goes me down the drive
Into the house and into bed,
And when Santa peeked in and saw a bush sleeping
He just laughed and shook his head.

I'd forgotten to take off my disguise,
So my bed was full of leaves and limbs
But I think ol' Santa thought I was asleep
'Cause I got lots of gifts from him.

But that Terrible Gerrible struck again,
And that candy plate was clean.
And my Christmas poem to my wife
Instead of saying *beautiful* said she looked like a *bean*.

LAUGHTER

But I'll get him next year, you'll see,
I won't let him get away.
But now it's back to my new 'lectric train,
Merry Christmas and have a good day.

Part 3

LOVE

A MARRIAGE OF GOLD

The vows have been said, the bouquet will be thrown,
and when at last, you're together, alone,
remember this wedding was the easy part,
now, newlyweds, the marriage has to start.
If you want to make it together, as long as you live,
you need to learn to easily say, "I'm sorry, I was wrong, I forgive."
Because in time wrinkles will come, the chest begins to sag,
this race you started together, at times will begin to drag.
That's when you must reach deep inside, and let commitment take control,
and see how this silvery, shining wedding will turn into a marriage of gold.
So, let me leave you with this thought you can take with you to the end,
remember you're each other's lover, best supporter, ally, and friend.

THE WORDS I'VE SAID

If one of you ever says something that causes hurt in the other's heart,
remember this isn't their usual style, and don't let an argument start.
Just say, "I know this isn't like you, What else can be troubling you?
Maybe I took your words the wrong way, take my hand and let's talk this through."
Because by the door your enemy is waiting, seeking marriages to devour,
but if you make "I forgive" your motto, those times can be your greatest hour.

FOR MY BRIDE

Two sets of slippers, side by side,
One for me, the other, my bride.
A preacher spoke, and the people cried,
Some for me, some for my bride.
She is my choice, my want, my pride,
So soft she sleeps, she sleeps, my bride.
I touched her cheek, while she slept, I cried,
She doesn't know how I love my bride.
The only thing they should inscribe
Upon my grave, is *For Her He Died*.

THE WINNER

What are the chances
of me meeting up with you,
in this people-packed planet
of about a billion or two?

The odds are greater still,
that it could ever be,
that if I would love you,
you would ever love me.

LOVE

Maybe I was just lucky,
perhaps it was all God's plan,
but I came out the winner
when you accepted my hand.

WARMTH TO THE SNOW

Leaves dancing on the wind
geese pressed 'gainst the sky
heavy clothes and mittens
kind of make me cry

It's sad seeing a year end
knowing as each go by
I have fewer winters left
till I close shop and die

But having you beside me
adds warmth to the snow
and makes each winter bearable
I just thought you ought to know

FORTY-TWO

Forty-two years old, you say?
So, what has she done with her life?
Well, for twenty-one of those forty-two years
She's been my loving wife.

She's properly raised our two kids,
Nurtured them in the Word of the Lord.
She's been able to prepare banquets,
When beans were all we could afford.

Her hair now may have a hint of gray,
But her eyes still have that gleam.
And her legs, oh those legs, that turned me on,
Still walk through all my dreams.

She's become my teacher, my counselor, my friend,
And the number one encourager of me.
She gave me the gift of fatherhood,
With the finest kids that ever could be.

But mostly what she's accomplished,
That I'm so proud of on this day,
Is every morning she takes my hand
And joins me when I pray.

GOD BROUGHT YOU TO ME

I'm so glad God brought you to me,
a man filled with hurt and fears,
you healed the hurt and lifted me,
you gave me the strength to have tears,
and though it's like it was just yesterday,
we're now working on our twenty-seventh year
and I don't wonder what heaven is like,
with you I have heaven right here.

LOVE

MY VALENTINE

She kissed me with her eyes
and caressed me with her smile
How little I knew then
That in what seemed a little while
She'd taken over my heart
Bewitched or maybe beguiled
Either way mattered not to me
As I went gladly down the aisle
My friends said, *It'll never work*
He is such a woman-hater
But they were wrong, we're going strong
These forty-five years later
And since each day with her
Is better than the day before
I can't wait to get up each morning
So we can love each other more
So thank You, Lord, for giving me
This woman so sweet and fine
And may she for years to come
Still be my valentine

FOR THE 48TH

A young man and woman fell in love
not knowing the true meaning of,
or the demands their love would endure,
those times in the dark when they'd think, are you sure?
But still their love was greater than
temptations for any other woman or man,
and years would come and years would go,
and their love continued to grow and grow.
Their lives and love would so mesh
they truly, truly became one flesh.
Now there are wrinkles and a few scars,
but when they stand at night and look at the stars,
there is still that tremor in their touch,
and the desire is there just as much
as when love filled them both with bliss,
and the fire still erupts when they kiss.
So what do we do with all this time and all these miles?
For our forty-eighth anniversary, I think we'll just smile.

ME WITHOUT YOU
for our forty-ninth anniversary

Like a bird with no song,
the summer sky with no blue,
or a flower with no fragrance,
that is me without you.

Like a child with no laughter,
or early spring with no rain,
all these are me without you,
please let me explain.

I was an empty vessel,
a broken piece of a man,
with no help or no hope,
then you took my hand.

LOVE

At first I thought it was a dream,
for how could a girl like you
take the time and my brokenness
and make me better than new.

Your trick it seems was simple.
You gave me unconditional love,
with a tenderness I can't explain
matched only by God above.

Now after forty-nine years,
I still can't believe it's true,
but I know I am nothing,
except when I'm with you.

A KISS ABOVE ALL KISSES

Soft on my lips
was the taste of her smile
a kiss above all kisses
that would linger a while
I didn't know then
how long it would be
that her kiss above all kisses
would be given to me
now I'm old and cranky
but nevertheless
she still fills my heart
I have been so blessed
and that kiss above all kisses
I am so happy to say
will be waiting with her
when I come home today
and that first lingering kiss
given when I first met her
after fifty years of practice
has only gotten better.

YEAR FIFTY-TWO

It seems our race together is slowing down
Still the end is not quite in sight
So I want to make the next few years
The greatest we will have in our flight
I want us to look back remember and laugh
Maybe we'll even share a tear or two
'Cause I don't regret one moment since we met
Our life has been beautiful because of you
When people see us still together
Two old fogies deeply in love
They can't imagine how I got you
They say what was she thinking of
Perhaps I caught you in a moment of weakness
Maybe it was my charm, my humor, my glib
But maybe God planned it all
Like Eve for Adam, you were my rib
Whatever the cause that brought us together
What held us together was you
And our race just keeps on getting better
As we celebrate year fifty-two.

FIRST LOVE

We always remember our first love,
at least this is what I've been told.
The memory of that first love lingers
until we are way beyond old.
Now I don't know if that is true,
about your first love from the past,
all I remember or care about,
is that you, darling, are my last.

ONCE I DIDN'T LOVE YOU

Once I didn't love you
once I didn't care
once it didn't matter
if you were really there

Once wedlock seemed to me
like misery, toil, and strife
like an anchor on my future
like giving up my life

But now it seems that I was wrong
I can't believe I was so blind
the chains and shackles I thought you were
were only shackles in my mind

The chains that made me a prisoner
as passive as a dove
were welded by your heart
and each link was made of love

SHE TOUCHED ME

She touched me this morning
more by what she said than did
And opened up a part of me
I thought I'd carefully hid
She asked me if I was hurting
I tearfully told her no
She again uncovered some of me
That I didn't want to show
She asked if she could love me
For today, tomorrow, and all time
She kissed tenderly my damp cheek
Then put her hand in mine
Trust me she said softly
Let yourself be free to care

But my mind's warning system
Played loudly again *Beware*
But something in her eyes and touch
Her gentle ways and voice
Crumbled all of my resistance
I really had no choice
So I bared to her my naked soul
Made available to her every part
And she this morning touched me
And started mending for us my heart

WHEN I WAS YOUNG AND STRONG

Can you remember when I was young and strong?
No, well, neither can I.
But there must have been such a time
for me to have caught your eye.
You must have seen potential in me,
that has kept you here this long.
Whatever was that spark, hope, or dream,
It must have been super strong.
Because after years of struggling to make it,
I still haven't found the gold.
The only riches that I have acquired,
is your heart that I hold.
And this gray hair and wrinkles I possess,
that cause me great concern,
you say, to you, it couldn't matter less,
they're highlights of life's pages we've turned.
So if I can't remember just how it started,
there is one thing on which you can depend,
for the rest of the time I'm with you,
I'm gonna make it memorable till the end.

HOLDING YOU

If heaven ever came to earth,
if only for a moment or two,
to let us see all the beauty
our eyes are allowed to view,
If the heavenly choirs and orchestras
played only where we could hear
and taste the sound that we found
lingering in our ears,
If the greatest of God's good designs were here,
and He has designed more than a few,
I know here deep in my heart,
I would be holding you.

REMNANTS OF MY MIND

I found the remnants of my mind
a couple of days ago,
but what have I done with it now,
I don't really know.
I guess it doesn't matter much,
the thoughts in it were so few,
best I can recollect,
all it had in it was you.

HER PRECIOUS MEMORIES

I was sitting in my favorite pew
just about to doze off,
when almost like a whispered prayer
came a voice from the choir loft.

THE WORDS I'VE SAID

It sounded like the peal of a bell,
or a bow on a violin string,
so I raised my head and eyes expecting
to see an angel with halo and wings.

I saw it was an old gray lady
whose husband had recently died,
but there was no sadness, just praise in her
as she sang to God in Whom she relied.

"Precious memories, how they linger,
how they ever flood my soul."
She paused and said, "Thank You, Lord,
for the years I had Jim to hold.

"You gave me the best You ever had,
when Jesus died on Calvary's tree,
but it was a close runner-up
when you gave Jim to me.

"We never really had a lot of things
that rich folks are so proud of,
but You gave us children and children's children,
and fifty-three years of abundant love."

She started again to sing softly
"I come to the garden alone,"
then smiled and said sweetly
"but I'll soon be going home."

"And knowing Jim, he's busying himself
giving our home it's final loving touch.
And he'll carry me 'cross the threshold again,
thank You, Lord, for giving so much."

I hadn't noticed but I had tears
gathered in the corner of my eyes,
for the words that she sang and said
had caused me to realize

LOVE

That with the time I have left
every day for the rest of my life
I'm gonna say "I love you,
and thank God that you're my wife."

NO ONE BUT YOU

I know sometimes that it may seem
I've something on my mind.
And you may think I'm not with you,
And I know from time to time,
I've caused you to doubt the depth of my love
When my gaze is fixed and clouded,
But it's not someone else I'm thinking of,
It's my own worth I've doubted.
Being a man, I must be strong,
Never bending, I must succeed.
But sometimes I doubt I'll make it,
I haven't the strength I need.
A man provides for his children and bride
Over failure he must rise above.
So these blank stares only hide my fears,
There's no one but you I love.

SHE GAVE

She helped me out of my insecurities
She brought me up when I was down
When I was weak, she became my strength
When I went astray, she turned me around
She gave me courage when I was fearful
And from our union she gave new life
She's given me more than I ever hoped for
She's my greatest gift, she's my wife.

FOUND HEART

Did you leave your heart here,
Perhaps so I could find it?
I noticed that it's all broken,
Let me try to bind it.
I will tenderly care for it,
I'll locate every missing part,
Then wrap it gently with my love,
And attach it to my heart.

NEW LOVE

When my heart was broken
I prayed, Lord, let me die
the one who said I'll love you always
always knew that it was a lie
but the Lord in His goodness
ignored my plea and gave me life
and sent to me a new love
and this new love became my wife
I guess she could still break my heart
toss me out in the pouring rain
but after all these years of us together
having her would be worth the pain.

UNREQUITED

Though uninvited and unrequited,
his love for her never waned.
And through the years and through the tears,
time and again he explained.

LOVE

I know she'll probably love me,
just like I've always loved her.
Given the time, I'm sure that I'm
going to see her feelings stir.

But in the end, it was as a friend
when he said his final goodbye.
At her death he had nothing left
except to sit alone and cry.

Sometimes no doubt things work out,
and sadly sometimes they don't.
Sometimes it seems what we dream,
the things we truly want,

slip away from our grasp
and fall through our fingers,
leaving no trace they were there at all,
but oh, how the memory lingers.

I WAS GOING TO SAY

I was going to say thank you
I was going to say I care
I almost said I love you
Then suddenly you weren't there

Now just to have you with me
There's nothing I wouldn't do
If only once more I could say
Dearest love, I thank you

DID YOU

Did you know what to say
when he said that he loved you?
Did you ever let your feelings show?

When he said he would never
put anyone above you,
couldn't you let him know?

When he said he would die
if you were to leave him,
did you think about your power?

When he begged you to stay,
and you knew it would grieve him,
did you grant him one final hour?

When he called you that night
to cry to you goodbye,
did you have to rant and rave?

When he fulfilled his promise
that he'd rather die,
did you even stop by his grave?

SILLY MOON

Silly moon, silly star
they both wonder where you are
but I don't

Silly cloud in the sky
thinks of you and starts to cry
but I don't

LOVE

Silly dreams fallen apart
now someone has a broken heart
but I don't

Someone has you and the love you'll give
and will have you as long as they live
but I don't

IN MY MEMORY

I taste the sweetness of her kiss
feel the dampness of her tears
but only in my memory
she's been gone for so many years

her laughter echoes through me
her voice wakes me at dawn
but only in my memory
so many years now, she's been gone

only one touch, one taste, one time
so how could it possibly be
that she has so entrenched herself
in my memory

I see her wave goodbye to me
the train whistle rings in my ears
but only in my memory
she's been gone, I think, for years

HANDS

Her hands were small, mottled, and thin,
His hands were big, calloused, and old.
You could almost see through her skin,
But these were the hands he loved to hold.
There was a time back in their prime
When they both were young and strong,
Those hands would only touch briefly
As the two would walk along.
There was a nervousness in his hands
That warm day in early spring,
When she extended her hand to him
As he placed on it a ring.
Then came years of their hands working together,
Changing a wedding into a marriage,
Building a home and life together,
Hands rocking a baby carriage.
He raised his hands in a salute
As he headed off to war.
Hers waved good-bye at the train station,
Not knowing what they were fighting for.
They brushed tears away from their eyes
At the same station when he returned.
And their hands began to show aging
From the life lessons they'd learned.
They swung their partners as they danced,
They folded their hands together in prayer,
And worked together raising their children,
Who knew their hands were always there.
But on this night in the fading light
He gently kissed her hand
Saying, "I know it's time for you to go,
And I'm trying to understand.
Just tell Jesus when you arrive,
I know this is what He planned,
But if you can wait just inside the gate,
I'll be along soon to hold your hand."

LOVE

PATHS

I'll run with you awhile, she said,
 until we reach the end.
So young in love, heart in heart,
 they took off like the wind.

I'll walk with you awhile, she said,
 some years on down the road.
As time and toil and labor
 had them a little bent and bowed.

I'll rest with you awhile, she said,
 at evening I heard her say.
Come lay your head on my breast,
 we've come a long, long way.

I'll sleep with you in a while, she said,
 here next to your bed of stone.
And I thank God that on all our paths,
 we never had to walk alone.

TO BE OR NOT

To be or not to be,
was Shakespeare's question.
But there is more to be asked,
here are a few suggestions.
Why don't rainbows fall,
How can bumblebees fly,
Why sometimes does laughter,
Make us sometimes cry,
Why does music touch us,
Deep inside our hearts,
Where do roads end,
How does love start,
Why do the ones we love
Unexpectedly leave,

Or how can a broken heart
Learn not to grieve,
Why do couples grow old together
To be separated by death,
And still whisper I love you
With their last dying breath?

THE WIDOWER

Her fragrance lingered long
so very long after she was gone
and our children's laughter echoed
till well after they were grown
now as I sit here alone this evening
I miss them more than you can know
but my wife and kids are with me
seems like everywhere I go
I'm aware my time here is running short
but you know I don't mind its end
because I'll be with her soon
my wife, my lover, my friend

DUSTY OLD HEART

I'm going to shake out my dusty old heart
and try to love again,
to see if I can feel the warmth
I felt way back then.

After your death I locked my heart
and placed it on a shelf.
I swore to never bring it out,
to live all by myself.

LOVE

But now Martha, after all these years
I really feel alone,
and I need someone to talk to,
someone to share a home.

I've met someone who makes me smile
like you used to do.
She's sweet and kind and thoughtful,
I think you'd like her too.

I know she'll never take your place,
and I hope you'll understand,
she helped fill the void you left,
but I'll always be your man.

She says she really loves me,
and I think she probably does.
What we'll have will be something special,
but not like ours was.

So now, Martha, I'm going to try it,
whether I lose or win,
I'm going to shake out my dusty old heart
and try to love again.

I LOVE

I love happy endings,
all silly and sappy and sweet.
I love when the underdog is victorious
over the team that can't be beat.

I love to see old couples on a stroll,
laughing and still holding hands.
I love to hear those yesteryear songs
from my youth's favorite bands.

THE WORDS I'VE SAID

I love to watch fireworks displays
on holidays like the Fourth of July.
I love to see winter coming
with colored leaves spotting the sky.

I love the smell of bacon cooking,
or cookies beginning to bake.
I love the summer sun's warmth
against the coolness of a lake.

I love so many, many things,
it seems indeed I do,
but of the things I mostly love
truly, I mostly love you.

THE FRONT PORCH SWING

The squeak of the chain on the front porch swing
as it sways in the wind,
brings to mind a long-lost time
when we were more than friends.

How many times did we sit and talk
of our dreams and plans and things,
your hand as soft as a shadow in mine,
on our magic carpet, our front porch swing.

Oh, the times we flew through space
to the far-off worlds dreamed of,
and the first feather-soft kiss you let me steal,
how it carried us into love.

We raised our family in that swing,
with gladness I still recall,
sleepy heads on our shoulders at night,
so young, so loved, so small.

LOVE

That front porch swing saw them grow
to maturity from a child,
and that swing must have carried each of them
about a million miles.

They've now moved away with young of their own.
I miss them, but they've done the right thing,
and since the night is young and pretty as you are Momma,
let's you and me go swing.

SMILE

The beauty and dignity of old men
The excited expectancy of a child
The warm embrace of close friends
These things make me smile

Folks giving out food on holidays
To those whose lives have been a trial
Rainbows shining after the rain
These things make me smile

Church chimes ringing on Sunday morn
Echoing their hope for a while
Sunsets all pink and blue and gray
These things make me smile

Grandmothers with children on their laps
Homecoming kids in the latest styles
Nervous and flowered trying to dance
These things make me smile

So many things make me smile
I should never wear a frown
But when I'm tired or hurting
When I let my guard down

I find my face is stressed and worn
From some thoughts I let run wild
I need to remember that God loves me
And this alone should make me smile.

FOREVER HERS

She was a 10th grade cheerleader,
he was in her algebra class.
He wrote hundreds of notes to her,
none he had the courage to pass.
Just to walk by her in the hall,
he'd go out of his way.
He chose a locker next to hers,
hoping he'd be able to say,
"I think you're cute. I think you're great.
You're something special to me."
All he got out was about algebra,
and why A plus B equals C.
She looked at him and kinda smiled,
and touched him on his hand.
In that one brief contact
... the boy became a man.
"Could you, I mean, would you
go to me with the show?"
Again she smiled that perfect smile,
and said that she would go.
He didn't really need to shave,
but he needed that Aqua Velva Blue.
He washed and cleaned the family car
till it looked practically new.
Two movies that night at the drive-in
designed to draw her near,
a comedy with Martin and Lewis,
a chiller-thriller... "Cape Fear."
He placed his arm on the back of the seat,
planning to draw her close.
Just as she turned to him to speak,

LOVE

there they were nose to nose.
This was what he'd hoped for,
the mood, the time like this,
but he just stared in her eyes,
afraid to try a kiss.
Later at her door that night,
she touched his face with her fingertips.
She smiled and said, "Good night."
and kissed him full on the lips.
He didn't remember the drive home.
It was the kiss he was thinking of.
He was by all medical evidence,
totally smitten with love.
She dated others that year,
but he never would.
He was forever hers.
He was in love for good.
By the time senior year came around
everyone knew one thing,
they would be together forever.
They had each other's rings.
She had his with tape on her finger.
He wore hers on a chain.
They planned out their lives together,
but sometimes plans change.
She went off to college,
He went off to Viet Nam.
She said she would wait for him,
but he never made it home.
Somewhere in the jungle,
their teenage dreams died.
Somewhere in a dorm at night,
she held his ring and cried.
Later on, she would marry,
raise a family, have a career,
and sometimes alone she'd remember,
the boy of her teenage years.

ONE MORE

One more smile
one more laugh
one more selfie
photograph

one more day
of us together
one more step
toward forever

one more page
in our memory book
one more time
our love will look

one more reflection
on our life that's been
one more time
I'd love to live it again

FOR A LITTLE WHILE

For a little while he was ours.
For a little while he was here.
For a little while we held him.
For a little while we shed a tear.
For a little while we were hoping.
For a little while we longed to see.
For a little while we felt him growing,
Wondering what all he would be.
For a little while there was laughter.
For a little while there were smiles.
For a little while we knew him,
This darling, my sweet fragile child.
But God in His great wisdom,
Who only wants for us His best,

Took him to be with Him in heaven,
Where our child will be so blessed.
For in that heavenly nursery
He can crawl upon Jesus' lap,
And wait for our arrival,
Perhaps rest there, take a nap.
Yes, for a little while he was ours.
For a little while we wanted him to stay.
But we didn't just love him for a little while,
We will love him now and for always.

LOVE WHEN YOU LIVE

"You there, who perhaps,
Knew him best,
Might say a word for him,
Here where he rests."
I shifted my weight,
Wanting to sit,
Scratched my worn jeans,
Sniffed, blew my nose, and spit.
"What do you say 'bout a man
You never know'd?
He was a stranger to most men,
But a friend to the road.
He worked most the fall,
Odd jobs on the place,
And now that death
Lies on his face,
All I can say are the words
He always lived by,
If you love when you live,
You'll live when you die."

FRIENDS

You could see them together
Hiking the high trail,
One a laughing girl,
The other a wagging tail.
All these years together,
Mere minutes now it seems,
This girl and her dog,
Each living a dream.
There was no greater love
In the whole world
Than the love they shared,
This dog and her girl.
She discovered that
On her bluest day,
This dog's smile
Could carry her away,
To rolling laughter
And yelps of glee,
Pleasant, how pleasant
Is the memory.
Yet the heart will hurt deeply
When one's friend is gone,
Leaving the other
To take those trails alone.
But I believe this to be true,
... In fact, I will bet,
That sadder still is the one
Who has no dog to forget.

TELL HER

What do you say to a girl that's five
you're smart, you're beautiful, you're so much alive
do you say almost shyly I love you
do you giggle and say this gift is for you
do you hold her and tell her that most of all

LOVE

she's filled your life though she's tiny and small
do you tell her of life with all its delusions
or of the future with wondrous illusions
do you tell her this love is from mom and me
'cause you're more than we ever hoped you'd be
do you tell her you love her and how you'll grieve
when she meets her love and has to leave
do you tell her how you'll hold her close
when you give her away with a wedding toast
do you tell her without her you'll be always alone
when she's grown and married and finally gone
do you tell her you love her more than your life
you tell her all this and you tell your wife.

WORDS

TRUE...
words can hurt
words can heal
change the way
that we feel
touch our hearts
touch our souls
leave us hot
leave us cold
but...
the right word
in the right place
leaves a smile
on my face
this is especially
TRUE...
and why I love
to hear a word from you

WHO I WAS WHO I AM

That is who I was,
but it's not who I am.
I now have compassion,
I used to not give a damn.
The bottom of the bottle
was the only thing I sought.
I never took time for others
in the manner that I ought.
I thought I had no value,
no reason for my birth.
I felt if I drank enough,
I'd escape the bonds of earth.
That is who I was,
but luckily for me,
I changed my direction
toward the man I would be.
You see a little bit of God's grace
will go a long, long way,
and throw in a loving spouse
and children to brighten the day.
My journey isn't over yet,
but I am well on my way,
and whenever I feel I'm slipping back
I stop and take time to pray.

TESSIE

It was easy to like Tessie Mae Wilcox, but it was easier to hate her. Well, almost. I spent most of the tenth year of my life doing one or the other.

For those of you who knew her, let me refresh your memories. For those of you who didn't have the displeasure of meeting her, allow me, by way of a word picture, to introduce her to you.

Tessie Mae Wilcox was her name, and we were neighbors. This was when I lived in Beulah Flats, Mississippi. Her parents were divorced, and she and her mama came to live with her mama's mama.

LOVE

The first time I saw her I was scattering cracked corn for the hens so I could gather eggs for breakfast.

"What'cha doing?" she asked.

I looked up at this spindle-legged girl hanging on the fence. Her hair, red and stringy, seemed almost ablaze in the morning sun.

Before I had time to answer, which I most certainly was not going to do, because any fool could plainly see what I was doing, she said, "My name is Tessie Mae Wilcox. I'm eleven years old. I live here with my granny now, and you just stepped in a pile of chicken mess."

I felt the sticky wetness between my toes and turned about three shades of red as I hopped one-legged over to a patch of grass to wipe my foot.

"What's your name?" she asked, not waiting for an answer. "You're kind of puny looking, you know. Bet you got worms. My mama always gives me a tonic for worms. If you want, I can get her to fix you some."

Her questions and answers came in a rapid-fire succession before I could even think or answer.

She finally paused to breathe and said, "I don't have a boyfriend here yet, but I might let you be my boyfriend, if you want. But then maybe I won't," she said as she hopped down from the fence and ran back to her house as her mama called.

I gathered the eggs and took them in for breakfast, talking to myself all the time.

"The nerve of that girl. Thinking I wanted to be some ol' girl's boyfriend. Even if I did, I sure wouldn't pick some redheaded motor mouth."

Mama said, "Who were you talking to out there?"

"I wasn't talking to anyone. I was listening to some new girl next door."

"Why, I bet that's Lillian's granddaughter," Mama said. "She told me her daughter and granddaughter were moving in. Such a shame for Lillian, her daughter being divorced and all. Now, Sledge, I want you to be especially nice to that young lady. Why she's probably scared to death, what with the divorce, the move, and having to start a new school. Tell you what, honey, after breakfast we'll go over and get properly introduced."

Whenever Mama called me "honey" it generally meant I was going to have to do something I didn't want to do. And I didn't need to be any more introduced than I already was.

I knew as sure as it was Saturday, that I'd be the one elected to walk Miss Motor Mouth to school.

THE WORDS I'VE SAID

"But, Mama, this is the only day I have to do things. Between school and church, I only got one day for myself after my chores."

"You only 'have' one day," Mama said, correcting my grammar, "and on this one day you're going to share it. You might make a new friend."

"Yeah, and frogs fly," I said under my breath.

"What did you say?" Mama asked.

"Oh, yeah, I'll try," I said and gave her my best smile.

The thing about my mama was that when she was head up on me doing something, I better well get it done. My mama could whip harder than anybody in the whole state of Mississippi, I believed. Course, I really hadn't been whipped by anyone but Mama and Papa, and Papa couldn't hold a candle to Mama when it came to a whipping. But I'm getting away from my story. Let me just say I knew my Saturday was shot.

Miss Lillian, Tessie Mae's grandmother, and my mama were best of friends. Mama fixed Miss Lillian's supper for a week when her husband died, and Miss Lillian was always bringing some fresh canned something or other for Mama. I swear our pantry was about to split open with jars from Miss Lillian.

After Mama and Miss Lillian said their hellos, I was formerly introduced to Miss Lillian's daughter and granddaughter.

"Tessie Mae, I'd like you to meet my son, Kenneth L. Strickland."

I stuck out my hand and let it drop when she just stared at it. I guess she thought she might catch worms or something.

Miss Lillian said, "I have a pot of tea brewing and some cobbler cooking. Won't y'all stay for a while? You young'uns can visit and get to know each other."

Tessie Mae jumped on that idea like a frog on a fly.

"Yes, let's do! Kenneth, let me show you my room. Do your friends call you Kenneth? I like that name. It's kind of strong sounding."

"No," I said, "everyone calls me Sledge."

"Sledge?" she laughed. "You mean like in sledgehammer?"

"No," I said. "Sledge, like in Sgt. Sledge Carter, G-man. He's my favorite in the serial we watch each Saturday morning at the New Joy Theater. When me and my friends play Junior G-men, I am always Sledge Carter. And I always get my man."

"Well, Sledge," Tessie grinned, "I'll try to remember that, but I think Kenneth sounds more romantic."

I felt my face flush. "I'll show you something I'm working on," I said, changing the subject.

"OK."

LOVE

"Mama, Tessie and me are going back to the house. I want to show her my racecar."

"Tessie and I."

"Yes, ma'am." My racecar, which I had built without any help on design or materials, was a real beauty. It had a long board, about twelve inches wide for the bottom, a peach basket nailed on its side for the hood, and a legless chair I'd found, nailed to the board for the seat. It was sitting up on some firewood so I could attach the wheels as I found them. There were three wheels on it. All I needed to find was the last wheel and it could be tested.

"This doesn't look like much of a racecar to me," said Tessie Mae. "It looks like a peach basket and a legless chair nailed to a piece of board."

Obviously, Tessie Mae knew nothing about racecars.

"Anyway," she continued, "the land's too flat around here to use that thing 'less you pull it behind somebody's car."

"Well, 'Miss Car Expert,' I happen to know where there is a giant hill, almost a mountain, not too far from here. I'll test it there."

The mountain probably was more like about one hundred feet high, but exact height seemed unimportant since my creation was being challenged.

"I'll believe it when I see it," she said.

That Monday I was, as I had feared, ordered to walk Tessie Mae to school.

"OK, Tessie Mae, this is what we'll do. When we get to school, we'll be on the back side of it. We'll split up, and I'll go on around to the front first, then you come on in. If any of my friends see me walking with some girl I'm not kin to, I'll just about die."

Tessie Mae agreed to that, saying she certainly wouldn't want to cause me to about die.

When we got to the school, I ran on ahead around the corner to where my friends always gathered as we waited for the bell.

"Hey, Billy," I shouted as I ran up, "how was the trip to your aunt's?"

"Aw, it wasn't so bad," Billy said, "matter of fact..."

Before he could finish his sentence, Tessie Mae came walking around the corner of the school. She paused and looked around, first toward the front door then over to me and my friends.

She gave this dumb old smile and shouted, "Hi Kenneth, Honey, I mean Sledge," and started walking toward us.

Billy said, "Kenneth, Honey?" and started rolling with laughter. All the boys were giggling. I was turning about three shades of red.

THE WORDS I'VE SAID

Tessie Mae walked over to me and reached up and hugged me and said, "See you after class, Sugar," then turned and disappeared into the school.

By this time, Billy and the others were about to wet their britches from laughing so hard. The only thing I could do was, after school, I'd have to run away. Maybe I'd join the circus or just ride the trains like I heard about hobos doing. But I knew that if I lived till I was grown, I'd never, ever be able to survive in the same school with Tessie Mae Wilcox.

The bell rang calling us to class. At least, I thought, in here my friends couldn't give me any grief about Tessie Mae. Someone, though, had already come in and written in big letters on the black board "SLEDGE LOVES RED!" I swear I thought I'd pass out from embarrassment. I didn't see how it could get worse. Shows how shortsighted I was.

The door opened and in walked Tessie Mae. Seems like when her folks were divorced, she missed a lot of school and studies and was having to repeat a grade.

"Everyone," Mrs. Carlisle said as she read the note handed her by Tessie Mae, "this is Tessie Mae Wilcox. Let's all make her feel welcome. Now, Tessie Mae, if you'll take a seat, we'll get our math books out and get started."

As Tessie Mae walked back to her seat, she patted me on the head. The class erupted in laughter and shouts of "Sledge loves Red! Sledge loves Red!"

"Alright, everyone!" Mrs. Carlisle said. "Enough of that! Now let's get to our studies."

Well, you can just imagine how school was from then on. It was almost more than a body could stand.

Tessie Mae always seemed to make better grades than me, and she could outrun me at recess, and she delighted in doing things to me in front of my friends just to watch my face turn about three shades of red. She delighted in coming over to my house after school and discussing schoolwork with my mama.

"Mrs. Strickland, how did Sledge do on the math test today? I made a ninety-four on it," she'd say.

"Why, I didn't even know he had to take a test today. He was out looking for parts for his car yesterday with one of his friends."

"Oh, Sledge," Mama called "how did you do on that math test today? Tessie Mae made a ninety-four."

"I... uh, got just under an eighty on it, Mama."

"How far under?"

"Well... about thirteen points."

LOVE

Mama snapped, "You mean you only made a sixty-seven? Well, we'll not be working on your car tonight, no siree! You'll be studying your math and that's final."

"Good night, Mrs. Strickland, Sledge," Tessie Mae said with a twinkle in her eye.

I believe that the serpent from the garden had been reborn in Tessie Mae Wilcox.

Sometimes though, when no one was around but the two of us, you know, she could be right civil. She told me about how she felt rejected by her father when he left her mama. She said it must have been her fault. I told her I didn't see how a grown man would leave because of something his kid had done. If he did, he wasn't acting very grown. Sometimes at night, we would sit in the limbs of this old Chinaberry tree between our houses and talk about the stars and space and what we wanted to be when we got grown. I wanted to be a racecar driver, or else a G-man, or maybe both. Tessie Mae said she wanted to be someone's wife.

"A wife forever and ever," she would say with a look of sadness in her eyes.

Still no matter how decent she was when we were alone, she seemed to delight in finding new ways to embarrass me in front of others. About the time I'd promise myself to strangle her with her own red hair, she'd up and do something kind of sweet.

This embarrassment at school was just about more than I could take though. Thank goodness school finally ended for the summer. No more "SLEDGE LOVES RED" all over school. I'd get some rest at last because Tessie Mae was going to visit her daddy for the summer.

"Sledge," Tessie Mae said, "I came by to tell you goodbye for a while. I'll be leaving in the morning at six. Mama's taking me to the bus station. I'll be writing you sometimes this summer." I looked at her, and she had that same look of sadness in her eyes that she sometimes had when we talked privately.

"Well," I said, "you have a safe summer. I'll try to finish..."

Tessie Mae grabbed my face in both her hands and pressed her lips tightly to mine. My eyes must have been about as big around as jar lids. I'd never seen a girl that close before. I'd never been kissed by a girl before. I felt my face start to turn about three shades of red.

I put my hands on her shoulders to push her away and was amazed at how soft she felt. Something inside of me quit pushing, I guess. I didn't have the strength to push her away. Matter of fact, I was weak as a kitten. My knees started shaking and my ears got a roaring sound in them like when you listen to the ocean in a seashell.

THE WORDS I'VE SAID

The kiss, which seemed to last for months, lasted only a second or so, but it was incredible. It wasn't the passionate kisses that I would discover later on, but it was my first kiss from a girl.

With that, Tessie Mae spun in her tracks and ran into the house.

I lay in bed that night and pressed my fingertips to my lips trying to recapture the feeling, but it couldn't be done.

She was gone when I awoke the next morning. I fiddled with my car and went to visit Billy, but something wasn't right.

"Durned ol' girls! Who needs 'em?" I said.

All Tessie Mae did all year was embarrass me, yet now I wanted to shout out loud that she had kissed me.

"Durned ol' girls! Who needs 'em?" I said repeatedly.

But at night, I would look for the light in her room in the house only to see darkness.

"Durned ol' girls. Who needs 'em?" ... Maybe me.

THE KID

way back then when I was ten
and she was five or so
a skinny kid from down the street
followed me wherever I'd go
I couldn't run her off
I couldn't make her leave
I couldn't get rid of her
and now would you believe
I'm twenty-nine, she's twenty-four
and to show how things have changed
today at five at our church
I'm going to change her name
that skinny kid from down the street
all pigtails and knobby knees
is dressed like an angel in white
and taking the breath out of me
what a sweet surprise life held
who would have thought when I ran and hid
that one day I'd ask her to stay forever
today, when I marry the kid

LOVE

CHRISTMAS TREASURES

Christmas treasures, poems and pieces,
That through the years I've kept,
Some of these I laughingly received,
While over some others I wept.

A ring from an older aunt,
Priceless, but not of gold,
A crayon-colored Christmas card
From the hands of a four-year-old.

A silver set, a syrup pitcher,
Some things too personal to mention,
And goofy gifts from my sweetheart
But bought with good intentions.

A Bible from a group I taught,
A calico cat made of clay,
And lots of love and laughter
Given on Christmas day.

But the gift I treasure most of all
Wasn't under a Christmas tree,
It was fragile and small, in a cow's stall,
God gave His Son to me.

This gift came from the great I AM,
And it came before I was.
But it's not a gift for me alone
But for everyone because

God so loved the entire world,
A world that was hopelessly lost,
That He gave to us Jesus His Son
To be nailed to a wooden cross.

So that all who believe in Him,
Those who accept this gift of love,
Will live eternally with Jesus
In heavenly homes above.

My treasure chest holds earthly gifts
Of poems, and pieces and parts,
But God's gift of perfect love
... I keep in my heart.

GIVING AND FORGIVING

Christmas is the time for giving and forgiving,
so as we celebrate Christ's birth,
we need to remember that it was God's forgiveness
that brought Jesus to earth.

This gift of Christ that God gave us
was for the forgiveness of our sin,
a way to enter a holy relationship
and become the Son of God's kin.

Jesus said it, His life displayed it,
His prayer taught us to forgive.
Leave all vengeance to God alone,
forgive if we want to live.

Now as we share Christmas with family and friends,
remember when Jesus was crucified,
He said, "Father forgive them,"
and to teach forgiveness is why He died.

LOVE

THE OLD MAN'S CHRISTMAS

The old man watched the shoppers moving,
and they all seemed to glow.
He smiled to himself and started home
turning his collar to the snow.
At home by the fire,
over his teacup he seemed to gaze
at her memory and past Christmases
that danced in the blaze.
He thought of those past Christmases,
of the joys and gifts they had known,
and wondered how this one would be
now that she was gone.
This would be his first without her,
and since all their children were grown
and scattered across the country,
he'd have to face Christmas alone.
Of course he'd call all their kids
and wish the grandchildren well,
but her Christmas morning kiss he'd miss
more than he could tell.
The old man's calloused trembling hands,
wrinkled by the ages,
reached and took his old worn Bible
and slowly thumbed the pages.
Now where's that verse, he said to himself,
the one we learned together,
that one that brought us warmth
no matter what the weather.
His eyes held for a moment,
as a smile crossed his face,
he read, "You are never alone
for I am with you always."
The old man drifted off to sleep,
dreaming of Christmases he had left,
and a bearded young man with nailed scarred hands
gently held him as he slept.

A STRANGE OCCURENCE

Could this occurrence have been any stranger?
In the form of a baby, hope was born in a manger.
The creator of all, giver of life and breath,
Came in a cow stall to conquer sin and death.
Breastfed and diapered the same as you and me
Except he'd been around for an eternity.
God's Son, the King of Kings, wrapped in this helpless child,
Hope, light of the world, yet born meek and mild.
Born for one purpose, to walk among men,
God in human flesh came to pay for our sin.
From a babe in a manger to Golgotha's tree,
He may have come for all but He died for me.
Knowing the degenerate sinner I was,
He could have done this only because
He loved me more than heaven above
And wanted me to know God's perfect love.

GOD TO MAN

From infinite God to infant man
from a cow stall to Calvary
from Bethlehem to Jerusalem
Christ came to Earth for me

From Heaven's throne to a wooden cross
from a gold crown to one of thorns
from perfect God to a bloodied body
Christ, for me, was born

From sin's death to my salvation
from imprisoned to a soul set free
from true love and true love only
Christ provided all this for me

LOVE

From deafness I was made to hear
from blindness I was made to see
that from before the dawn of time
Christ planned to rescue me

So from infinite God to finite man
to death on a cross from a lowly stall
for my debts that I could never pay
my Lord Jesus has paid them all

Part 4

LIGHT

SET FREE

Hey bartender, I'll have another,
I'm celebrating because I'm free!
I was prepared to be crucified,
yet the people cried to release me.

The things I've done, the sins I've committed,
and still I've been set free.
Instead they took a man I don't know
and nailed him to a tree.

I can't understand what happened,
I have no earthly idea why,
but for some reason, somehow, I'm now free
because that young man had to die.

Yes, bartender, I am Barabbas,
I know you've heard my name.
If there were any rules or laws, I broke them,
I earned all my black-hearted fame.

THE WORDS I'VE SAID

But hold up on that other drink,
I won't be needing that anymore.
I've got a strange feeling inside,
something I've never felt before.

I don't know what's happening to me,
in all of my life I have never cried,
yet I broke down and sobbed like a child
when that young man finally died.

For years I've been a customer here,
but I won't be back again.
There are so many people that I've wronged,
I want to see them to make amends.

YOU SAW ME

When Caiphas gave Jesus over to Pilate, falsely accused, to be tried,
to be whipped, tortured, degraded, and later to be crucified,
through that bloody crown of thorns, what do you think Christ could see?
Oh! My God! I ask forgiveness, I know that You saw me.

When the Roman soldiers stripped Him bare and pierced Him through His side,
and gambled for His garments, while His mother and brothers cried,
as that hammer raised to drive the spike that nailed Him to the tree,
in the face of that Roman soldier, Oh, my God! You saw me.

When the sky grew dark and angry, and crying winds blew and blew,
and the earth trembled in its agony, and the veil was torn in two,
with His dying words, "Father, forgive them," who did He look down to see?
Oh, my God, in Your forgiveness, I know that You saw me.

THEY HUNG HIM THERE

They hung Him there for all to see
On two pieces of timber hewn from a tree.
They scourged and beat and spat on Him,
And then they nailed Him to the limbs.
How Satan must have laughed with glee,
And thought that from Jesus he was finally free.
And that he had Jesus where He belonged.
And you know, Satan was both right and wrong.
Wrong that from Jesus he was free,
But right that Jesus belonged on that tree.
Wrong in thinking that he had won,
Wrong that he had killed God's Son.
But Satan didn't realize how right he was
When he had Jesus crucified, because
Christ's crucifixion was really God's plan
As the only salvation for sin-filled man.
And though sin hung Christ on that tree
He hung there freely for you and me.
The only reason He came to earth
Was to give us all a chance for new birth.
Where we could shed the shackles of sin
And through His death we could win.
So Satan's greatest hour of infamy
Was also Christ's greatest victory.
So remember the crucifixion cross
Brought Satan his greatest loss,
And gives opportunity to the sinner
For a heavenly life... let's stay with the winner.

A MOTHER'S POINT OF VIEW

I knew I shouldn't have worried,
but what's a mother to think,
we'd come so far, and He wasn't with us,
my heart began to sink.
We went back and found Him,
and was my face ever red,
'cause young as He was, in front of others,
to me, His own mother, He said,
"Why did you come seeking Me?
You know you shouldn't have bothered.
You of all should know that I
would be about the business of My Father."
Now I know what you mothers might think,
that I had a real uppity Son,
but you see He was very special to me,
He was a very special one.
He was just like His Father
in all of the deeds He'd done,
but I nursed Him at my breast,
and He was my very first Son.
I knew He had lots to do,
He tried so often to make me see,
no matter how big He grew,
He was still my baby to me.
I couldn't believe the violent outrage,
the horrid things both said and done,
how they attacked and wanted to kill
this my precious Son.
Now I know He was just like His Father,
and He had thousands flock to see
Him walk and talk and heal and teach,
... but He was still my Son to me.
So I know, mothers, you will understand,
perhaps even feel my loss,
and know exactly the hurt I felt
as they raised Him on that cross.
I know He was His Father's Son,
and His death was planned from the start,
but He was my first, and His dying
simply just broke my heart.

THE HARDEST COMMAND

The hardest of God's commands,
to do, to practice, to live,
is a single word worth repeating,
forgive, forgive, forgive.

SOMEONE PRAYED FOR ME

My spirit was almost broken,
Misery was all I could see,
But somehow I was encouraged
Because today, someone prayed for me.

The problems I faced seemed like mountains,
Or at least a pounding sea.
I could have easily been destroyed by them,
But today, someone prayed for me.

I even contemplated death
As an escape from my misery,
But instead I chose to carry on,
Because today, someone prayed for me.

Someone prayed for me today,
Giving me the strength to see it through.
I may never know who it was,
But perhaps it was you.

You may feel your prayers are wasted,
The results you may not see,
But my life now is much richer,
Because today, someone prayed for me.

Reprinted and used by permission by Lifeway.

HE CANNOT

There is no problem so big
That He cannot bear it,
There is no pain so great
That He cannot share it.

There is no weakness
That He cannot strengthen,
There is no shortcoming
That He cannot lengthen.

There is no darkness
That He cannot brighten,
There is no blindness
That He cannot lighten.

There are no fears
That He cannot assure,
There are no illnesses
That He cannot cure.

There is nothing
That He cannot afford,
All things are possible
With Jesus my Lord.

THE INVITATION

You are cordially invited
To come home with Me.
To meet My Father
And live eternally.
To share the bounty
He provides for thee,
And all you need do
To RSVP
Is simply to trust
And believe in Me.
With love,
Jesus

PRODIGAL'S FATHER

Whether my child comes early
or whether my child comes late
or whether my child never comes
I'll still be waiting at the gate

HE ANSWERED WHO

When Satan sought permission from God
to attack Job to see what he'd do,
God allowed Satan to take all Job had
except his life, because God already knew
that Job was a man of God,
a rarity because there were so few
who would trust God's love completely
no matter what He allowed Satan to do.
Satan said Job will turn away
and reject the God whose love is true,
and seek false gods to worship,
maybe make a false idol or two.
But Job never rejected his God,
although his hurt broke his heart in two.
And when Job finally asked God why,
He didn't answer why. He answered Who.
"Where were you when I hung the stars
or split the darkness and light in two,
and separated the water from dry land,
and with my breath gave life to you?
Answer me, O Man, if you can,
when you look at all that I do."
Job was left without a word to say
because he knew God's words were true.
And that God is God, and Job was not,
Neither am I, and neither are you.
So don't be surprised when you ask God why
And he doesn't answer why. He answers Who.

A CARPENTER'S SON

He can make a way where there is no way,
Build up hope where there is none.
He can create new hearts from broken bits,
But after all He's a carpenter's son.

His gate is straight and narrow,
His yoke is light enough for everyone.
He mends the broken, lifts up the lonely,
But after all He's a carpenter's son.

There are many mansions where He lives,
Why, He's even saving me one.
He's got nail scars on His hands and feet,
But after all He's a carpenter's son.

Just a carpenter's son, no more than that,
Though I know it may sound odd,
But Jesus, this son of a carpenter,
Is also the Son of God.

Give a Christian an inch
and they'll tell you about their Ruler!

WHEN STEPHEN WAS STONED

Stephen was full of grace and power
And performing all wonders and signs
But the men from the synagogue
Sought whatever means they could find
To run him out or run him off
To kill him if it need be
Because the powerful message Stephen proclaimed
They wanted no one to ever see

So that day they stoned Stephen to death
And as he died there in the sand
Jesus, when He saw Stephen's faith
Was so moved He decided to stand
Now for Jesus the Christ who reigns over all
Who sits at God's right hand
To become so moved by someone's faith
That He simply has to stand
Is really beyond my comprehension
But I would love one day to see
That my walk, and talk, and actions, and faith
Would have Jesus standing for me

RAINS

"You're nothing but an old fool,"
to Noah his neighbors said.
"All this talk of impending doom,
you're completely out of your head.
There's no need to build an ark.
You serve an unseen god in vain.
We'll drink and dance on your grave."
... and then came the rain.

"Who does he think he's talking about?"
the Pharisees and Scribes began to fuss.
"If his followers continue to believe him,
they'll be able to see through us.
He equates himself with God Almighty,
claiming to be one and the same.
We'll rid ourselves of him on the cross."
... and then came the rain.

"I don't need any God of yours,"
an acquaintance said mockingly.
"I'm a millionaire, own my own business,
and I owe my success to me.
Your God's for weaklings and losers,
a crutch for the emotionally lame.
My limo's waiting, I've got to hurry."
... and then came the rain.

Yes, the rain came in Noah's time,
and on Golgotha the rains did fall.
And the rain will come in your life and mine,
and really drench us all.
But how we fare in this storm,
whether we're uprooted or stay in place,
will depend on if we've anchored ourselves
to Jesus Christ's life-saving grace.

REVIVAL

Tell you folks what we need here
Is an old-fashioned revival
A podium-pounding tent shaker
About eternal survival

This laid-back preaching we been getting
With its soft and satiny tone
Says Jesus Christ is oh so nice
He's a lamb upon the throne

Now I don't deny that Christ is nice
But I know one other thing
He may have been a lamb for the slaughter
But He's coming back a King!

LIGHT

He's a King who'll finish a war
He started a long time ago
And there won't be any in-between
We gotta let people know

You'll either be for Christ the King
Or in Satan's satanic troop
And the war'll shake the world's foundations
Like a cur dog shakes a boot

Now we already know who will win
It's spelled out in the Revelation
So let's draft some more for Christ's team
Just to help in the celebration

We need to explain it loud and proud
Till everybody's heard
That Christ the King is coming back
We can take Him at His Word!

We need to get people's attention
With our every ounce of breath
'Cause the war will leave behind two things
Eternal life or eternal death

So let's tell everybody about the war
Let's not miss a single one
And we'll have that old-fashioned revival
As soon as the battle is done!

A HOMECOMING

"Welcome home, Son," His Father said
and embraced Him tenderly.
"We've got so much to talk about,
come, sit right here by Me."
"I don't know where to start, Father,
there's just so much to tell.

THE WORDS I'VE SAID

I made a few friends while I was there,
but mostly it was pure hell.
I'm afraid at times I became frustrated
because I just couldn't make them see.
They're so used to believing the competition's lies,
only a few really trusted in Me.
I'd walk and talk and meet the folks,
there were thousands I spoke to.
But they never totally grasped the truth,
well, except for maybe a few.
But these few, Dad, you'd really like.
Paul, and Mathew, and all the rest
were simple men when we first met,
now they're strong enough for any test.
And, oh, how tested I know they'll be
because that place is so full of sin.
But they'll pay the price, even lay down their lives,
if for only one soul they win.
I saw John while I was there,
and with him I realized
how great Your love is, Father,
when we're truly, spiritually baptized."
The Father smiled again at His Son
as ten thousand thousand fell to their knees.
And He repeated words the young man already heard
"This is My Son in whom I'm well pleased."
The Father continued talking to Him,
And with a sad and heavy sigh,
He said, "I'm sorry, Son, I turned away,
but, I just couldn't watch You die.
You did everything I asked of You.
You've shown the truth and borne the shame.
They've heard Your voice, now it's their choice
to feel the love or feel the flame."

PRAY AGAIN

When your back is against the wall,
When you've finally had it all,
Don't give up, don't give in,
Just one more time, pray again.

When you've prayed the night through,
And you see nothing change, nothing new,
And you wonder where God has been,
Get back on your knees and pray again.

When the hurts fester, and the pain is intense,
When giving up makes perfect sense,
And the sky is blacker than it's ever been,
Wipe away those tears and pray again.

Pray again, and again, and again,
Never give up, never give in,
The answers will come in the end,
So lift you voice and pray again.

THE PLANETS' LIGHT

The planets travel around the sun
As everybody knows,
And at night they're seen sparkling
As bright as any star that glows.

Yet these planets have no light in themselves,
Their light is not their own.
Without the sun to give warmth and light,
These planets would die alone.

Oh, how like the planets we are
As we travel through time and space.
We sometimes sparkle brightly,
As light shows in our face.

But let's give credit where credit is due.
This light we're speaking of
Is not something we create ourselves.
It's a reflection of God's love.

God gave this light to brighten our lives,
It's a strength we can use.
But God doesn't force us to reflect it,
It's up to us to choose.

We can exist forever in darkness
Or live forever in light.
I've made my choice and now rejoice,
Jesus shines in me tonight.

PERHAPS SOON

Perhaps soon, too soon it could be
you're lying there, or perhaps it's me,
with family gathered, maybe some friends,
saying their goodbyes to us at the end.
Hopefully the words over us read
will describe us as gone but not as dead.
Though the body is empty that we lived in,
we will be more alive than we've ever been.
So say we are with our Father above,
the giver of life, the giver of love,
the One who gave us our first breath,
and who stopped our last in what we call death.
Say that we've only gone away,
and that we will meet again one day.
When your time is up and He calls your name,
when at last you leave your earthly frame,
and look upon our dear Lord's face,
and step into His sweet embrace,
we'll be there standing in line
to say welcome home, friend, you did just fine.

THE MAN OF GOD

His old tired body finally gave out.
The Man of God had died!
And thousands lined the highway
as he took his final ride.

He was a common, simple man,
known by all, all over the world.
Tall and handsome to many,
but attracted to only one girl.

He was called, set apart by God,
to preach the Good News to the world.
And he faithfully carried out his mission,
as year after year unfurled.

He was the greatest preacher I ever heard.
He made the truth easy to know.
I know his words changed my life,
those many, many years ago.

But today the Man of God is dead.
He is now present with the Lord.
And people wonder will there be another
who can so passionately preach the Word.

Will God bring up another Billy Graham?
Skeptics would say chances are few.
But I know God has another warrior.
Who knows, perhaps it's you.

Here's the direction to enter heaven's gate
turn right at Jesus and just go straight

TALITHA KUM
Mark 5:41

Jesus said, "Talitha kum," which translates,
"Little girl, I say to you arise!"
And my mother stood, leaving her body in the bed,
and went to meet Jesus in the skies.
I hated seeing her leaving,
but was happy for her release.
She left this troubled, toil-filled place,
to move on to eternal peace.
She'd been tired for so long now,
after all these years she deserved this rest.
And I know that for all who knew her,
their lives were truly blessed.
Though her leaving did bring us sorrow,
I know we'll be seeing her again.
She'll be waiting for us in heaven,
and probably have hot biscuits in the pan.
So good-bye, dear sweet mama of mine,
you're now in Jesus' tender care.
Just keep the porch light on for us,
soon we'll meet you for supper there.

COMFORTABLE

Like an old sweater, a pair of gloves
or your favorite easy chair
you know that when you're in them
comfort is waiting there
makes me kind of wonder though
if it just might be
that Christ who lives in my heart
is comfortable in me
if I'm not right in my daily life
if I neglect daily prayer
my mouth and actions might make me
uncomfortable for Jesus to wear

LIGHT

I'D RATHER

I'd rather have the lowest corner in heaven,
Than the highest throne in hell.
I'd rather have a smile from Jesus
Than all the praises Satan can tell.
I'd rather be considered earthly poor,
Having nothing but the Lord,
Than to own a thousand worldly treasures
Or all that Satan affords.
I'd rather be scolded by Jesus
Than have Satan say, "That's nice."
I want nothing from Satan but the recognition
That I belong to Christ.

BLACK FRIDAY

He got up on Sunday morning,
shook the dust from His hands.
He had died on Friday,
for the sins of every man.
He had a few people to see
before He went on his way.
His work was now finished.
He had no need to stay.
He was leaving us a helper,
in the form of the Holy Spirit,
available to every person
who would listen, who would hear it.
I think what touched me the most,
of all the wondrous things He'd done,
was from the cross He asked for forgiveness
for all of us who daily kill God's Son.

CHRISTMAS FEELING

The trees stand shivering in the December wind,
their leaves having long since flown.
The gray of darkness closing in,
another year is almost gone.

Church bells are ringing far away,
sounding both joyful and forlorn,
as the new snow softly sings along,
Hallelujah, the Christ Child was born.

Christmas, the time we celebrate
as the anniversary of Christ's birth,
seems to have a calming effect
on the grumblings of this earth.

Now wouldn't it be good, if everyone could,
fill their pockets with Christmas cheer,
instead of fussing and cussing and hurting each other,
they'd have this feeling of love through the year.

So this Christmas season let's all agree
to ask for help from the Lord above,
that we can keep this feeling of Christmas,
yet give it away all year wrapped in love.

CHRISTMAS INVITATION

They see the lights and tinsel
the gifts all around the tree
they see lots of smiling faces
I wonder if they see Me

They watch the annual parades
the football games on TV
they invite their neighbors in
I wonder if they invite Me

LIGHT

They sing along with Christmas carols
in some sort of harmony
and love to hear from friends far away
I wonder if they hear Me

I can't make them see Me
or make them invite Me in
or listen to My fervent call
to turn them away from sin

Just like opening up those presents
lying under the Christmas tree
they can find life's greatest gift
if they will only look for Me.

A CHRISTMAS POEM FOR DANA AND TERRY

Many years ago, in a far-away land,
Was a great big forest with trees tall and grand.

The trees stood tall nearly touching the sun
And played with the clouds, all except one.

One small tree cowering below
Had started out right but had failed to grow.

And often in the forest laughter rang
As the tall trees played, laughed, and sang.

But the small tree, "I'm afraid," often said,
"If they don't like me, I wish I were dead."

And the years would come, and the years would go,
And the big green trees continued to grow.

But the small tree sat and never grew,
And the clouds and the stars, it never knew.

But late one cold and wintry night,
All the trees stopped and looked at a light.

A single star in the heaven gleamed
That made the trees want to sing.

They didn't know why but they felt better,
And this was strange for this kind of weather.

Brothers walking by braving the snow
Were following the star, amazed at its glow.

They'd heard tell of a King of kings,
A Lord of lords to whom gifts they should bring.

But they were poor and had nothing you see,
So they stopped when they reached the smallest tree.

"What do you think?" one said to the other.
"It's more than we have, so let's take it, my brother."

So the smallest tree was taken with them,
And they placed tinsel and colors and beads on its limbs.

And hung it with holly and as all could see,
This short lowly bush was a beautiful tree.

Wise men and kings moved so the Babe could see,
As the poor boys brought in their gift, the tree.

And the Babe smiled as though He never would stop,
And the bright star in heaven settled on the tree's top.

Angels sang of joys to come, and Mary and Joseph could see,
That Jesus, Child and Savior, had had the first Christmas tree.

So that's why at Christmas you'll always see
In the center of all gifts, a Christmas tree.

THE FATHER'S CHRISTMAS GIFT

Back before the dawn of time
before the era of man
God saw our shortcomings
and came up with a plan
He took the One who was always with Him
and I'm sure with a tear-filled eye
sent Him to earth to be born as a baby
not only to be born but also to die
this babe in a manger so very long ago
a small soft and fragile thing
would grow to shake the world's foundation
would become the King of Kings
and now about two thousand years later
we still celebrate His birth
and remember in songs and pageants
His short walk upon the earth
but at this time we also need
to remember His death there on the cross
and three days later He rose from the dead
so His followers would not be lost
so sing hymns of praise and hallelujahs
have peace and goodwill to all men
and let's live our lives for Him our Savior
until we are with Him again
happy birthday sweet Jesus
bless You for all You've done
and eternal thanks to You our Father
for the Christmas gift of Your Son

THE SHADOW OF A CROSS

In Bethlehem, in a manger,
Wrapped in swaddling cloths,
A baby born to Mary and Joseph
Lay in the shadow of a cross.

In the excitement of the moment
This one thing was almost lost,
That on the face of the fragile child
Fell the shadow of the cross.

His feet and hands so tiny,
So perfect, so frail, so soft,
Would one day be pierced, spilling His blood,
In the shadow of the cross.

Now this shadow seemed unimportant
On this day of great celebration,
But years later it would prove to be
The door to our salvation.

The meaning of Christmas has been trampled under
By merchants till it's almost lost,
But I, for one, remember the Son,
Born in the shadow of the cross.

THE TURNING TIDE

The tide has turned here in the bay,
There is now no need for me to stay,
So I'll weigh anchor and be on my way,
With my back to the shore and my face to the spray.

I'll let the gulls guide me with their constant cry,
As they press themselves against the sky,
Caring not where they go and much less why,
Still I'll follow them till the day I die.

Then you can wrap in linen what's left of me,
Speak your words above and give me to the sea,
And from time to time in your memory,
In the crashing waves my face you will see.

INDEX

Family Photos

Page 3 – Author, age 3
Page 5 – Author with younger siblings
Page 11 – Author (on right in 1st photo, on left in 2nd) and others, Ed's Beach Service, Panama City Beach, Florida
Page 17 – Author and daughter; author and children.
Page 38 – Author's son
Page 39 – Author's daughter
Page 42 – Author's granddaughters
Page 45 – Author and daughter
Page 46 – Author and daughter
Page 62 – Author's sister-in-law, 1945
Page 74 – Author and sister and cousins, Opp, Alabama
Page 79 – Author and bride
Page 83 – Author and wife

Dobbins Chapel

I was asked by a member of the Chapel Foundation Committee to write a poem for the Rededication and Transfer of Ownership Ceremony in 2014 for the Dobbins Chapel. I was honored to do so and to have a copy of the poem hanging in this historic chapel at its beautiful new location.

ABOUT THE AUTHOR

Ted Harris was born on Christmas Day in the small cotton mill town of Opp, Alabama. He was born not in a hospital, but at home, so he could be close to his mama. This timing messed up his mother's Christmas dinner.

Ted is the oldest of four children, with two sisters, Sherry and Sandra, and one brother, Hal. They were all born in "LA," he and his two sisters in Lower Alabama, and his brother in Los Angeles. They moved a lot when he was young, so he was very shy and didn't make many friends. He does get back to Opp when he can to visit cousins and have the best Southern food in the world. And after all, it's on the way to Panama City Beach!

Ted has lived in the Atlanta area with his wife, Suzi, for over 52 years. Because of moving so many times as a child, Ted is happy to say he has lived for the past 45 years in the same house in Marietta. They have two children, Dana and Hunter, and two granddaughters, Carter and Spencer. For Ted, writing has always been a natural expression of his soul, inspired by his observations of life, his empathy, and later, his faith. He hopes that these poems and stories, set free from his pen, will make you think, make you smile, and reach your heart.